T0365296

Cambridge Elements ☰

Elements in Creativity and Imagination
edited by
Anna Abraham
University of Georgia, USA

MECHANISMS OF CHANGE AND CREATIVITY IN NATURE AND CULTURE

Arne Dietrich
American University of Beirut

CAMBRIDGE
UNIVERSITY PRESS

CAMBRIDGE
UNIVERSITY PRESS

Shaftesbury Road, Cambridge CB2 8EA, United Kingdom

One Liberty Plaza, 20th Floor, New York, NY 10006, USA

477 Williamstown Road, Port Melbourne, VIC 3207, Australia

314–321, 3rd Floor, Plot 3, Splendor Forum, Jasola District Centre, New Delhi – 110025, India

103 Penang Road, #05–06/07, Visioncrest Commercial, Singapore 238467

Cambridge University Press is part of Cambridge University Press & Assessment, a department of the University of Cambridge.

We share the University's mission to contribute to society through the pursuit of education, learning and research at the highest international levels of excellence.

www.cambridge.org
Information on this title: www.cambridge.org/9781009663144

DOI: 10.1017/9781009091701

When citing this work, please include a reference to the DOI 10.1017/9781009091701

First published 2025

A catalogue record for this publication is available from the British Library

ISBN 978-1-009-66314-4 Hardback
ISBN 978-1-009-09544-0 Paperback
ISSN 2752-3950 (online)
ISSN 2752-3942 (print)

Cambridge University Press & Assessment has no responsibility for the persistence or accuracy of URLs for external or third-party internet websites referred to in this publication and does not guarantee that any content on such websites is, or will remain, accurate or appropriate.

Mechanisms of Change and Creativity in Nature and Culture

Elements in Creativity and Imagination

DOI: 10.1017/9781009091701
First published online: April 2025

Arne Dietrich
American University of Beirut
Author for correspondence: Arne Dietrich, Arne.dietrich@aub.edu.lb

Abstract: This Element is about change. Specifically, it's about the underlying mechanisms that cause change to happen, both in nature and in culture; what types there are, how they work, where they can be found, and when they come into play. The ultimate aim is to shed light on two barbed issues. First, what kind of system of change is culture and, second, what kind of change in that system counts as creativity; that is, what are the properties of the mechanisms of change when we explore unknown regions of the cultural realm. To that end, a novel theoretical framework is proposed that is based on the concept of a sightedness continuum. A sightedness framework for the mechanisms of change can integrate the three mechanisms causing gradual, adaptive, and cumulative change – evolution, learning, and development – into a single dimension and provide a clear view of how they cause change.

Keywords: control systems, cultural evolution, prediction, sightedness, learning

ISBNs: 9781009663144 (HB), 9781009095440 (PB), 9781009091701 (OC)
ISSNs: 2752-3950 (online), 2752-3942 (print)

Contents

1 Introduction

1.1 A Preview of the Trail

This Element is about change. Specifically, it is about the underlying mechanisms that cause changes to happen, both in nature and in culture; what types there are, how they work, where they can be found, and when they come into play. The ultimate aim is to shed light on two barbed issues. First, what kind of system of change is culture and, second, what kind of change in that system counts as creativity; that is, what are the properties and characteristics of the mechanisms of change when we humans explore unknown regions of the cultural realm.

The trail we will take up to get a good viewpoint from which to see these issues is strewn with difficulties because it requires, at several mileposts, that we strenuously exert our imagination. But I promise it will grow on you the longer you stay with it. We will arrive at a first stretch when we reach a small platform from which we can appreciate a new theoretical framework. This novel structure is based on the concept of a sightedness continuum and establishes a direct and straightforward relationship linking the three general mechanisms that cause gradual, adaptive, and cumulative of change: evolution, learning, and development. The theoretical framework provides a powerful vantage point from which to see not only how these mechanisms of change cause change but also where and when these changes occur. It will also serve as a base for an examination of what kind of system of change culture constitutes and our efforts to look for creativity in that system.

From the trailhead below up to this first platform, there are several sights to behold. Early on, we secure a prevalent but often overlooked consensus position on cultural evolution, so that we can all stay together as a group. This includes sticking with the overall term of cultural evolution until we get ourselves into a position to quibble about it. In a sentence, this consensus is that human creativity, and by extension cultural evolution, is best characterized as an evolutionary process that has some coupling between variation and selection, or degrees of sightedness of the selection criteria. Because confusions and errors abound on this topic, it is critical for this novel theoretical framework that we have an unclouded understanding of what, exactly, is involved in neo-Darwinian and Lamarckian evolutionary algorithms in terms of sightedness. This part is familiar terrain and should not be controversial.

Once we have identified the blind-sighted dimension as the key to understanding the character of the system of culture, we will survey the prediction paradigm of neuroscience to extract two critical insights. One is a neural mechanism of how the human brain manages to get some sightedness of the fitness landscape when navigating what is supposedly an unknown problem space. In projecting hypothetical targets into that unknown topography, the brain's predictive computations put some sightedness into its thought trials, giving cultural evolutionary algorithms some unique properties, such as faster and more efficient heuristics and the ability to scaffold.

Second, we will also recast the process of learning from the sightedness perspective. Learning depends on prediction. It occurs in response to a prediction error, which, naturally, is a process that requires the existence of target information. Using these adaptive end points, the advances of the learner – the unit undergoing the change – is then instructed or directed. In other words, the changing unit has access, or visibility, to the selection criteria, making learning a fully sighted mechanism of change.

To render this insight clear and robust, learning – along with development and Lamarckian change later on – will be framed in terms of control systems engineering and Bayesian inferencing. Using the brain's motor control to work out the key computational principles, we will link sightedness to a control system in which the desired output is achieved by using a controller that directs the internal operations of the system. Since the opportunities to abandon the trail early are so numerous and the motivation to surrender to them is so strong, these cairns on the lower part of the trail will go a long way to block all the exists and stay the path.

Having equipped ourselves with sharper thinking tools, we now have a clear way forward. The novel theoretical framework invites the hiker to see the three kinds of mechanisms that cause change to come about – evolution, learning, and development – from a single dimension, the dimension of sightedness. In keeping all other complexities temporarily clamped, including interaction effects such as the Baldwin effect or evo-devo, the integration of all three algorithms of change into a unified axis can make visible links that can otherwise not be seen. For instance, when viewed in terms of sightedness, Lamarckian evolution should be reclassified as a learning process. Accordingly, Lamarckian evolution is a learning algorithm or, if you prefer, learning is a Lamarckian evolutionary algorithm. Throughout these lower parts of the trail however, we will refer to Lamarckian change as evolution until we can see the issue in the light of our novel theoretical framework.

Unlike in the blind, neo-Darwinian mechanism causing all the cumulative and creative changes in the biosphere, the fitness landscape in control systems is "visible" to the changing unit so that feedback from the selection criteria can instruct, or guide, the units undergoing the change. This visibility implies that these mechanisms of change can only work when the problem space is already known at the systems level. It also implies that they can use Bayesian predictive coding, among other computational tools, to bring about change.

Adopting the sightedness and control systems perspective brings out several other features and effects of the three mechanisms of change. One involves the location, acquisition, and transfer of controllers and what that means for problem spaces and sightedness values. Another involves different types of control systems. Depending on the feedback path, these are open loop control systems and closed loop control systems, which map well on to the processes of development and learning, respectively.

The new framework will become our guide for the higher sections of the trail. The joy of being high above the tree line is, of course, the panoramic view. This is just what we need for the next leg of our route, a systematic survey of the mechanisms of change in both nature and culture, as they appear from our novel theoretical structure. Once we understand how the crank mechanisms work, it is easier to tell where they can be found and when they come into play. For this task, we must distinguish in both systems of change – nature and culture – the problem spaces in which the topography is known, at least in principle, from those in which they are fundamentally unknown. The difference lies in the most general sense in the changing unit's "visibility" or "sightedness" of the fitness criteria, which, in turn, determines the type of algorithms of change that can be used to generate any change. Thinking through the resulting 2×2 matrix – system of change (nature versus culture) and problem space (known versus unknown) – is a task that requires discipline and vigor and that yields a satisfactory – and satisfying – account of the mechanisms and dynamics that cause gradual, adaptive, and cumulative change.

We now approach the summit of the trail and we can address our two barbed issues, which we will engage in reverse order. First, we will look for creativity. This search quickly becomes complicated for the simple reason that the brain's predictive processes generate partial sightedness even when the problem space is supposedly totally novel. To complicate things even further, there are also plenty of opportunities for creativity in principally known problem spaces, something that one might not suspect. To help clarify this, we will allot some space to the dual role played by prediction in known problem spaces.

From a few examples of how we humans discover, innovate, design, and create, we arrive at a general deduction about the mechanism of creative change. That is, there is a reciprocal causal interaction between sightedness, knowledge, and prediction. This reciprocal interaction implies that the creative process changes the mechanism of the creative process itself.

Finally, we can attend to the first barbed issue – what kind of system of change is culture? There are endless complexities attached to mechanisms of change that feature varying degrees of sightedness. And they make culture a system of change that is stranger and more fascinating than thought.

Anyone who has made it this far up the trail can now do more than just enjoy the conclusions arrived at after reaching the summit. The hiker can now also appreciate the details that get us there.

1.2 Directions to the Trailhead

If decades of fascinating discussions are any guide, most people who fail to make it to the summit do not give up along the way; rather, they do not make it to the trailhead in the first place. Heeding Woody Allen's observation that "eighty percent of success is just showing up," we must first acknowledge and clarify a number of undercurrents of resistance that shackle our imagination and thus prevent a general application of a neuroscientific, evolutionary, and algorithmic analysis of culturally changing systems. They must be identified and disarmed before we can comfortably start the journey.

The general aim of this preparatory work is to keep a lid on the anxieties that such a reductionist perspective induces and prevent them from depriving the hiker of the unfettered view that one has standing on the summit. We briefly touch on four of these recurrent misunderstandings.

One rather surprising form is resistance against neuroscience in general and involves the vague notion that the brain is not the only source of change in culture, creative change included. Accordingly, we must also consider social dynamics or the cultural context. What about creative ideas that emerge from people interacting during brainstorming sessions, for example? And what about embodied cognition, the idea that the body and its interaction with the physical environment also needs to be taken into account?

There is no need, however, to labor under this sort of neurophobia. As Henrich and colleagues (2008, p. 119) put it: "Culture can be understood in the most general sense as information stored in human brains." Social processes and cultural phenomena might very well be best explained by references to social processes and cultural phenomena. Nevertheless, they emanate from brains. In a brainstorming session, for instance, when people express their ideas, the creative change does not occur to the information in mid-flight between two people. Irrespective of how information gets into a brain – by way of genes, cultural environment, social learning, random events, and so on – changing the information into a novel combination occurs in the brain. To be altered, information still has to be represented in a computational system.

A second, closely related source of resistance is based on the lack of communication between those in the field of creativity and those in cultural evolution. A few exceptions aside, they do not talk to one another. In biology, there is no equivalent disciplinary boundary between the world of biological artifacts and the sources – genes – that generate, to a first approximation, all the artifacts of that system, including the mechanism of neo-Darwinian evolution that puts the information into those genes. In other words, geneticists and evolutionary biologists take from one another.

Those who study brains and those who study culture do not share in the same way. Neuroscientists working on creativity have nearly universally ignored the basic variation-selection rationale in setting up empirical protocols (Dietrich & Haider, 2017). All psychometric 'tests of creativity' collapse the two fundamental elements of the creative process, and it is hard to imagine useful neuroimaging data from studies blending variation with selection, given that both likely engage different cognitive processes and different brain areas (Dietrich, 2015). The same holds for those working on cultural evolution. There is a remarkable disconnect between the way we study the system of culture on the one hand and the underlying brain mechanisms that generate all the goodies of that system on the other. In this Element, we make a concerted effort to try to join the two.

The blanket rejection of an evolutionary approach to the study of culture, in any form, is perhaps still the strongest of all the recurrent misunderstandings. Therefore, it receives its own section, the next.

1.3 Basic Thinking Tools

Whenever cultural evolution is the topic, the temperature rises. Amidst the bruising rhetoric of ridicule and contempt on all sides, debates on how far Darwinism extends upward into culture typically generates more heat than light. Champions of Darwinism in culture like to describe their opponents as mushy humanists and soft-headed poets who, having overdosed on postmodernism, are prone to panic attacks whenever they hear the rattling of the saber of science. This being academia, it does not end there. Opponents heap scorn on the entire enterprise of Darwinizing the social sciences and humanities and like to depict their rivals as overzealous scientists and pigheaded technophiles who, having overdosed on reductionism, erratically swing the club of Darwinism at everything in sight.

There are some signs that the pugnacious hyperbole is subsiding a bit. Of course, there are those who regularly go into orbit denouncing Darwin outright – creationists, believers in intelligent design, and so on – but those people must be taken up elsewhere. We will focus here on neutralizing a third source of resistance, which is perhaps best called residual dualism. Apart from the study of consciousness, this residual dualism can be observed quite often when the topic turns to creativity and, by extension, cultural evolution. This resistance must be broached head-on, because any lack of clarity here is prone to lead to Cartesian danglers once we push for sound mechanistic explanations later on.

We all grow up with the warm blanket of dualism, the combination of instinctive truthiness and spiritual comfort that can only come from leaving your intuitions unexamined. Residual dualism fuels a tacit and deep-seated motivation to keep evolutionary and algorithmic thinking, in any form, out of culture and away from the mind. Efforts to protect the mind – and culture as its derivative product – from being a full member of the canon of science are nothing new. The irony is that residual dualists waste no time telling you that they have no qualms with Darwinism in biology. But after they cede the mind to be the outcome of evolutionary processes, they make a stance there and reject as absurd the application of the same principles to the mind. This is perhaps because they can dimly see that if the tug-of-war is lost here, at this line, there is nothing that protects our creativity, consciousness, and agency from a bad case of existential vertigo. Exactly where a residual dualist draws the line can differ greatly from one to the next but, eventually, if one presses hard enough, there is a line.

Residual dualists part ways, not to retreat into the walled enclave of vague Cartesian dualism, but because they misunderstand key terms and concepts. Common stumbles include conflating neo-Darwinism and Darwinism, being unclear about what is actually involved in a Lamarckian algorithm, the foresight fallacy, the argument from intention and purpose, or confusing ultimate (evolutionary) explanations that answer *why* questions with proximate (neural or cognitive) explanations that address *how* questions, all in the hope that Darwinism somehow goes away. Some confusions hit the same spot but from a different angle, and we will address some of them in the pages to come.

You can run but you can't hide, as they say. The snag with such motivated reasoning is, of course, that this defense requires, beyond said line, a miraculous force to make it all work. It is powerful proof that it is one thing to commit yourself to a view, it is quite another to accept all the logical consequences that go along with it.

Unfortunately, the most typical response to clarifying these issues is intellectual stonewalling. It is a disarming reflection of the determination to keep the Darwinian grenade from detonating inside the well-protected pocket in which we hold the mind and the cultural world it creates. Therefore, we make one more effort to address this form of resistance and offer in Figure 1 a simple sketch of why evolutionary thinking, for human creativity and cultural evolution, is a form of TINA (There Is No Alternative).

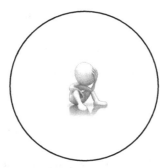

Figure 1 A commonsense illustration of culture as a basic Darwinian (variation–selection) system. Imagine you find yourself in the middle of an unknown problem space, the circle in this figure. The problem's solution is located somewhere in that space; but where? If you knew in which direction to go, creative thinking would not be necessary in the first place. So, how do you proceed? To start, you have no choice but to take a step, in some direction. But do you know if it is the right step, in the right direction? Of course not. So, you have to take several steps, in several directions. And there is your variation process! Naturally, some steps are good, some are not. And there is your selection process! The move you eventually end up making gets you to a new location (the inheritance process) and you are ready to do it all over again. In the universal language of mathematics, this sequence can be expressed in terms of a Darwinian (variational) evolutionary algorithm. Because of this, culture, the derivative product of the brain's action, can be said to evolve. Cultural units – however defined – are passed on leaving behind a trail of gradual, adaptive, and cumulative changes.

1.4 An Algorithmic Lens

A fourth and final source of resistance stems from a basic misunderstanding of what constitutes an algorithm. Our thinking is pulled out of shape here by the tradition, particularly in psychology, of believing that algorithms are said to differ from other problem-solving methods in fundamental ways. Supposedly, there are three kinds. The first is trial and error, which is claimed to be only really useful for problems that have a limited number of solutions. The second method is an algorithm, which is a strategy that proceeds by the strict application of a set of rules. Algorithms are foolproof if correctly executed, but they are also inefficient and require time. Suppose you lose your keys somewhere in your house. If you look for them using an algorithm, you would search the house square by square. Of course, this process is guaranteed to work but you may also go mad before finding them. The obvious, and misleading, conclusion to draw from this example is that humans do not use algorithms in daily life, because we must solve problems in real time. But luckily for us, there is a third method, heuristics. This is a rule of thumb, a sort of quick and dirty way of doing things, in which you start looking for the keys in the most likely places. It removes from the search a lot of seemingly foolish choices, leading to a speedier end of the search.

All three methods, however, are instances of algorithms. The trouble with this seemingly harmless way of illustrating the issue is that it invites the mistaken view that computers, being the mindless things they are, use mere algorithms while we are blessed with the gift of clever – meaning, heuristic – thinking and reflection. Failure to appreciate that algorithms can be heuristics has misled more than a few critics.

So, for simplicity, generality, and clarity, we adopt an algorithmic lens in this Element. Abstracting all three mechanisms of change – evolution, learning, and development – from their roots in, say, biology or psychology renders clear and robust important insights that are otherwise absent.

For instance, learning is a process that we typically associate with animals or humans acquiring information. But the deep-learning algorithms of computer programs demonstrate that the process can easily be abstracted from organisms. Likewise, we know evolution as a theory that explains life on Earth. But evolution need not involve genes, life, or ecosystems. It is a process that takes place whenever three conditions are met: replication, variation, and selection (Dawkins, 1976). As long as something, anything, shows variation, selection, and inheritance, that something, mindless or not, evolves. Evolution, then, is a general mechanism of change. Darwin's theory of evolution by natural selection, for instance, is a specific instantiation of the process of evolution. Neo-Darwinism, or the modern synthesis, which incorporates additional parameters in its algorithmic function – Weismann barrier, digital inheritance, blindness, genetic drift, sexual selection, epigenetics, and so on – is another. Lamarckian evolution can also be lifted from its roots in biology. Lamarck's theory of the inheritance of acquired characteristics, however, belongs to a different class of algorithms (Lewontin, 1970). It, too, represents a general mechanism of change.

2 Are You a Lumper or a Splitter?

2.1 Starting with the End

In what is known in engineering as a controller, we start this section with its conclusion. It is this. For all the – typically hot and overheated – debate on cultural evolution, a remarkably broad consensus has taken root. To a first approximation, the following is unanimously agreed upon: (1) Culture is an evolutionary system (Dawkins, 1976; Gould, 1979; Smith, 2013); (2) culture is a system with a variational or variation–selection pattern of change at the population level (Lewontin, 1991; Medawar, 1953); and (3) culture exhibits some coupling between variation and selection, or degrees of sightedness (Richerson & Boyd, 2005); that is, the brain's creative thought trials are not blind (Dietrich, 2015; Kronfeldner, 2010). Although we will suggest in this Element that adjustments be made to this consensus, it follows that cultural evolution, and by extension human creativity, can neither be described as a neo-Darwinian system with the added parameters of the modern synthesis nor a Lamarckian system that is based on a transformational pattern of change and thus on adaptation-guaranteeing instruction. Classifying culture as Darwinian or Lamarckian, then, is either a case of much ado about nothing or a tectonic shift in thinking, depending on whether you are a lumper or a splitter.

This point is widely underappreciated, so it is worth stressing. Whenever cultural evolution is the topic, discussions quickly become acrimonious and vociferous. Things can reach such a pitch that the emergence of a near-universal common ground in the theoretical landscape has largely gone unnoticed. But all parties agree that the basic grammar and logic of evolutionary thinking applies to the system of culture and that we generate creative ideas using a variation-selection process that has *some* sightedness. The goal in this section is not to establish this common ground – that's been done – but to block all the exists. In other words, this section covers mostly familiar (but often misunderstood) terrain and thus should not be controversial.

2.2 Was Darwin a Darwinist?

Darwinism to most people is the Darwinism of Darwin. This sounds like an obscure statement of the obvious but, as it happens, it is not. No sooner did Darwin hoist the flag of evolution, legions of biologists went to work on the nitty-gritty details of how this variation-selection drivetrain works. Darwinism as we know it now has become a much more restrictive and precise theory and is no longer the Darwinism of Darwin. This simple truth continues to be over-looked in even some of the most erudite and scrupulous writing on cultural evolution.

Darwin's theory was barely a few decades old when the first of the legions of biologists entered the picture and supplied for the first major twist in this tale. In the late 1800s, August Weismann showed that one type of cells only, germ cells (egg and sperm), carry hereditary information; all other bodily cells – somatic cells – are not agents of heredity. This genotype–phenotype distinction is the difference between the inherited basis of a trait and its observable expression.

The clincher was that the effect is strictly one-way. Since the germline holds the instructions to build somatic cells (and other germ cells), changes to them can ripple through to the next generation of somatic cells. Not so in reverse. With no means of making copies of themselves, bodily cells, neurons included, take any modification acquired in life into their molecular grave. Culture, in short, is not heritable, at least not biologically. The route – phenotype to genotype, and on to the next generation – is impossible. The Weismann barrier, as this is known, had two immediate effects. One, it put an end to Lamarck in biology. Duly sharpened like this, Lamarck's core idea, the inheritance of acquired characteristics, was consigned into the ever-fuller dustbin of biology's history. Two, it also put an end – wrongly, in this case – to Darwin in culture. Culture became seen on top of nature and any influence of biological processes on it – causal or otherwise – was flatly negated. This had consequences. For at this point, biologists and social scientists parted ways and stopped talking to one another, exceptions aside, for nearly 100 years.

If Weismann was pillar one, then Gregor Mendel was pillar two. Hereditary information can be passed on in one of two ways, either in entities that blend, like colored paint, or remain distinct, like tones in an accord. Blending inheritance was widely accepted in Darwin's time, even by Darwin. It was an inadequate model, however, and people knew it. It failed to explain, for instance, the simple matter of how some traits – blue eyes, say – can disappear for several generations only to reemerge down the line unaltered. In addition, blending dilutes variation, eroding the differences for natural selection to work on. Only a discontinuous copy mechanism could account for these phenomena, which is where Mendel's laws of heredity, rediscovered around the turn of the century, come in. In particulate Mendelian inheritance, genes from the parents stay as they are in the offspring; they do not mix. This is also called hard inheritance and contrasted with Lamarckian-style blending or soft inheritance. Genetics is, in a word, digital. Famously, Darwin did not know of Mendel's work.

These giant leaps, the genotype–phenotype distinction and the discrete mechanism of heredity, clarified two important components of the evolutionary system that propels the biosphere. In the 1930s, population genetics became the third major amendment to Darwin's original idea. The integration of all three improvements with Darwin's theory is known as the modern synthesis or, alternatively, neo-Darwinism (Fisher, 1930; Huxley, 1942).

The fact that Darwin's Darwinism is quite different from today's understanding of neo-Darwinism, with all the added bells and whistles of the modern synthesis, is a major source of confusion that plagues the modern debate on how far Darwinism extends upward into culture. All too often both sides in this face-off feed one another arrant hyperbole because they have a different take on Darwinism. I make an effort, therefore, to use consistent language.

2.3 Patterns of Change

Having identified, and broken off, that weary piece, we can now start unpacking this broad consensus. Historically, three dimensions have been used to define and classify evolutionary algorithms: First is the pattern of change at the population level – variational or transformational – that is, how change comes about in different evolutionary systems. Second is the coupling parameter – blindness or sightedness. Third is the method of inheritance, which can occur either by particulating units of information – the neo-Darwinian case – or by blending them – the Lamarckian case. Based on these, neo-Darwinism is variational, digital, and blind; Lamarckism is transformational, blended, and directed (Dennett, 1995; Gould, 1979; Lewontin, 1991; Mayr, 1981). A critical insight is that these dimensions need not come grouped together like this. An evolutionary algorithm can consist of a different mix (Kronfeldner, 2007). To jump before being pushed, this is the case for the evolutionary algorithms brains use to generate cultural change.

The first dimension (pattern of change) is the least contentious. How does a population, as a whole, change over time? A (neo-Darwinian) variational system is based on the variation-selection method. The constituent units of the system vary naturally and a sorting process biases their survival. Evolution occurs because different units have different copying rates, which shifts their relative distribution in the system. At the population level, this appears as a statistical change that alters the proportions of the different variants over time (Lewontin, 1970, 1991).

A (Lamarckian) transformational system is not based on variation but on adaptation-guaranteeing instruction. This generates a different pattern of change at the population level. A Lamarckian system knows no individuality, no variability, and no waste. Variation does exist but it is treated as noise and thus evolutionarily irrelevant. And without variation, a selection process is superfluous as there is nothing it could work on. Change occurs because all units of the system are transformed in lockstep, pulled into the direction of adaptation by instructions provided by the environment (Lewontin, 1991) (see Figure 2).

We should be clear not to equate Lamarckian change with creationism, however. The reason why it is always adaptive is not a divine power but rather the accessibility of the fitness values located in the environment. A Lamarckian algorithm is a lawful, instructive method of change that has no need for an intervening deity. But it does include, as a built-in feature, the notion of inevitable progress, the idea that there is automatic development toward greater complexity. Because change is controlled, or instructed, by the environment, it is sure to be for the better. This imposes a definite direction to Lamarckian

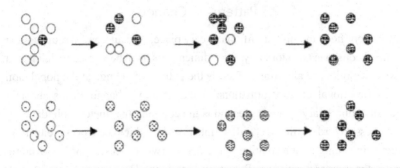

Figure 2 Patterns of change: The upper panel shows a Darwinian variational pattern of change. Individuals in such a system are unique. They vary. Evolution occurs because different types have different reproductive fitness, which shifts their relative distribution in the population. The lower panel shows a Lamarckian transformation pattern of change. This system has no variation and no selection. Change acts on every individual in the same way. Change occurs because the entire population is transformed together, pulled into the direction of complexity by the guidance of the environment (based on Medawar, 1953 64f).

change and gives it a purpose that doubles up as a kind of *ersatz* for a Creator. Put another way, the central feature of a Lamarckian system is the existence of target information that is accessible, or visible, to the changing unit so that feedback from it can pull all the units of the system toward the adaptive end points.

In engineering terms, this is known as a control system in which the desired output is achieved by using a controller that drives the internal operations of the system. You might have noticed that we are sort of making use of this method by starting this chapter, as we did, with its conclusion. A neo-Darwinian system does not have controllers because there are no targets. It can – but does not have to – lead to progress. Darwinian algorithms simply do what they do; they are creative – one uninformed move at a time – on their way to nowhere in particular.

The betraying sign of a variation-selection mechanism at work is waste. It is Exhibit A of the Darwinian argument: the waste that did not make it through the selection process. We can nudge a bit closer to seeing the Darwinian drivetrain behind human creativity by looking at the forensic evidence it would have to leave behind in the career paths of creators; things like splendid failures, messy zigzagging, serendipitous finds, descent with modification, dumb luck, useless contraptions, false theories, unsold paintings, or awful compositions. And of that there is plenty (Burke, 1995).

2.4 Degrees of Sightedness

The second dimension (blind/sighted) has been the eye of the storm from the very beginning. Of course, it has been the reason for Darwinism's noisy run-in with religion. It is not difficult to see why the utter lack of foresight and direction inherent in the (neo-)Darwinian variation-selection method causes existential vertigo in short order.

The many efforts to restore to evolution a guiding hand of higher wisdom in the variation component – directed mutation, notably – and the selection component – a force from above that handpicks the winners – are a disarming reflection on just how hard it is to go all the way with a theory of creation that lacks a teleological safety net. These positions quickly go boom because they merely postpone the place at which we must smuggle in the gift from the Gods.

The origins of our creative ideas, and how they arise, have been a prominent and long-standing showcase in this tug-of-war on cultural evolution. For the matter of blindness, the empirical research has often centered around evidence of what psychologists and computer scientists call expert systems. In a typical experiment of this kind the problem-solving habits of novices are compared to those of experts. After even a cursory glimpse at the results of such a study it is hard to escape the conclusion that the occurrence of novel ideas (variation) is influenced by the kind of problem (selection). Experts have acquired knowledge that allows them to generate guesses that are informed by the characteristics of the problem. This favoring of adaptability is a cognitive coupling between variation and selection and cannot be reconciled with Campbell's blind-variation-selective-retention (BVSR) model (see Campbell, 1960; Schooler & Dougal, 1999; Sternberg, 1998) that has been vehemently defended by Simonton (1999, 2010) until recently.

In the blind evolutionary algorithm of the biosphere, the twin subprocesses of variation and selection are discontinuous, with selection only imposing a direction on variation ex post facto, that is, after the variation process is done. Blind in this undirected – unguided or uncoupled – sense means that there is zero correlation between the factors causing variation and those that sort it; they are uncoupled. The Lamarckian algorithm, by contrast, is not based on variation, so blindness plays no role in it. It is a transformational or instructional system in which adaptation is guaranteed from the start by the environment. The probability that any change in it is adaptive is, therefore, 100 percent. Lamarckian change is fully directed or sighted (see Figure 3).

In nature, the evolutionary process obeys the neo-Darwinian algorithm. The Lamarckian algorithm does not describe biological evolution. This does not mean, however, that the Lamarckian algorithm cannot be found in nature. As we

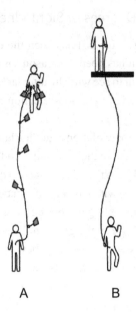

A   B

Figure 3 Lead versus top rope climbing: The fundamental difference between neo-Darwinian and Lamarckian change is the accessibility of fitness information to the units undergoing the change. To illustrate this in an oversimplified manner, consider the difference between lead (A) and top rope (B) climbing. On a new route (scenario A), a lead climber must ascend by trial and error. The climber is blind as to what constitutes an adaptive move on the way to the top, as the route has never been climbed before. It is an unknown problem space. Assuming for a moment an infinite number of routes up and an infinite number of rope teams, the overall pattern of change would look, from afar, variational in character. The matter is different for the climber who follows (scenario B). With the lead climber as an anchor on top, there is now a rope dangling down that guarantees a way to the top. The ascent of the second climber is sighted, as it can now be instructed using controllers generated by the lead climber above. The rope represents a control algorithm that eliminates evolutionarily meaningful variation and an infinite number of rope teams would produce, when seen from far, a transformational pattern of change.

will see once we get to our novel theoretical framework, it describes other adaptive mechanisms of change.

In culture, the matter is considerably more complex. However, a broad consensus has taken root recently based on the weight of the evidence from psychology and anthropology showing that human creating and designing is neither totally blind nor totally sighted (Kronfeldner, 2007; Richerson & Boyd,

2005). It is not blind because the occurrence of novel ideas (variation) is informed by the kind of problem as well as the knowledge of the problem solver (selection), and it is not sighted, otherwise creative thinking would not be necessary in the first place. Due to the partial cognitive coupling of variation to selection in the brain, cultural evolutionary algorithms possess degrees of sightedness (Dietrich, 2015; Dietrich & Haider, 2015).

Remember that Darwin did not know about this blind, ex post facto quirk of his theory. All his life, he accommodated Lamarck's idea of the inheritance of acquired characteristics and relied in his thinking in part on directed generation of novelty. It is fair to say, then, that Darwin did not think variation was totally blind. Ironically, those who demand that the evolutionary algorithm of the biosphere must be completely analogous to the one in the infosphere before we can legitimately apply Darwinian thinking to culture – neo-Darwinism, in other words – must be prepared, by the same token, to also defend the somewhat odd thesis that Darwin, believing as he did in blending and coupling, was not a Darwinist.

2.5 You Cannot Go There from Here

The third dimension (method of inheritance) is unsettled and will likely remain so for some time. This is because nobody has the foggiest understanding how the brain copies information. Neuroscience cannot even tell us how brains represent and store information, much less the copying mechanism. And with no knowledge of the brain's units of mentalese or the coding scheme, we cannot say if cultural transmission is a case of neo-Darwinian hard (digital) or Lamarckian soft (blended) inheritance, or indeed both, as it is entirely possible that both methods coexist (Dietrich, 2015). In consequence, we need to bracket this dimension, as it can only be settled by the neuroscientific counterpart of genetics.

Famously, Darwin was in the same fix. With no knowledge of particulate Mendelian genetics, the fundamental unit and mechanism of biological heredity was an intractable problem. In the same way that Darwin could only look at the phenotypical manifestations of change, we can only study the patterns of how actual cultural artifacts multiply, spread, and die. Picasso has evidently become the E. Coli of cultural evolution in this premature exchange of fire for his habit of signing and selling many preliminary sketches of his paintings (Simonton, 2007; Weisberg, 2004). But the brain mechanisms underlying cultural heredity cannot be gleaned from indirect anthropological and psychological evidence. We simply cannot go there from here. From one level up, all inheritance looks like blending, as any pattern of transmission can arise from any number of brain mechanisms. Still, we know that a blending process, and thus phenotypical adaptation, plays a role in cultural transmission, because cultural data sets show too much horizontal diffusion to fit mathematical models of population genetics which are based on a digital copying format (Richerson & Boyd, 2005). Luckily, we do not need to settle this matter in order to make progress on other fronts. As such, we leave the inheritance issue to one side.

2.6 Honing in on Sightedness

This analysis makes clear that the key to understanding the character of the system of culture is the blind-sighted dimension. In fully committing to degrees-of-sightedness thinking, the categorical reasoning that has dominated theorizing about cultural evolution – Darwinian versus Lamarckian, analogy versus disanalogy, digital memes versus soft blending, and so on – gives way to a fluid understanding that places neo-Darwinian evolution and Lamarckian change on a continuum.

It follows from degrees-of-sightedness thinking that the variational-transformational dimension must also be a continuum, as movement on the sightedness continuum results in corresponding change of appearance in the overall pattern of change exhibited by the system. That is, for any added degree of coupling between variation and selection in the evolutionary algorithm, the pattern of change, as seen from the population level, becomes ever more transformational in character. We can conclude then that the sightedness dimension (blind-sighted) and the pattern-of-change dimension at the population level reduce to one. More pointedly, the shift from a variational to a transformational pattern at the population level is a direct consequence of increased degrees of sightedness, as it is the sightedness dimension that produces the overall pattern at the (cultural) systems level. This was formerly only understood at the polar ends of this continuum, with full blindness generating a variational pattern and full sightedness a transformational pattern of change.

This reduction, in fact, requires us to make the first of several adjustments to the broad consensus we want to secure in this section – culture is a variational system with some sightedness. It is a conclusion based on the insight that evolutionary algorithms can be a mix of the classes variational/transformational and blind/directed (Kronfeldner, 2010). This, however, still contains the assumption that the class variational/transformational is a categorical one, with cultural evolution being one (variational), but not the other (transformational). But in the same way we cannot call the evolutionary system of culture blind, this reduction makes clear that we can also no longer maintain it to be a variational system. This dimension, too, would have to be expressed in degrees and placed on a continuum.

By identifying sightedness as the critical overall factor for our way forward, culture is recast as a highly dynamic and complex hybrid system in which a whole array of evolutionary algorithms with different sightedness values produce cultural change that shows up in all kinds of places on the variational/transformational dimension. Previously, culture has been thought of as a system that, like nature, should be definable by one specific type of evolutionary algorithm, at least on the three main dimensions of evolutionary algorithms. The tacit assumption that there must be one right evolutionary algorithm that describes the system of culture as a whole has surely contributed to the ferocity in the debate on cultural evolution. But once sightedness is placed on a continuum with (neo-Darwinian) blindness and (Lamarckian) directedness only occupying the ends, cultural evolutionary algorithms could fall anywhere on this continuum, probably exhibiting all degrees of sightedness in-between. The idea that the one evolutionary algorithm characterizing the entire system of culture does not exist or might be a moving target should inform mathematical models of cultural evolution.

2.7 What Is in a Name?

So far so good. What is less agreed on is how to classify this seemingly highly combustible view. At the very least, it exposes just how pointless the back-and-forth over the Darwinian or Lamarckian label is. Since culture is neither a neo-Darwinian nor a Lamarckian system, the issue of classifying culture as *Darwinian* depends primarily on whether you are a lumper or a splitter (Dietrich, 2015). A splitter equates Darwinism with neo-Darwinism and insists that all features of the modern synthesis must be present before the Darwinian label can be applied to culture. Since the coupling evident in human creativity is a breach of the central neo-Darwinian dogma of blindness, culture is not Darwinian. A lumper strips the definition of Darwinism to its basic core of a bottom-up, variation-selection process, which is Darwin's key insight after all. Since culture shows a strong variational pattern of change, culture is Darwinian. This can also be put in terms of sightedness or coupling (Kronfeldner, 2007). One can take zero coupling to be the lone member of the category of Darwinism and all degrees of sightedness to be members belonging to the category of Lamarckism. Based on this, culture is Lamarckian. You can also fly a kite for the exact opposite position, with 100 percent coupling being the sole constituent of the class of Lamarckism and all degrees of sightedness encompassing the class of Darwinism. Based on this, culture is not Lamarckian (see Figure 4).

Both positions are abusive. If you are a splitter you see the difference between biology and culture as evidence for two systems; if you are a lumper, you see

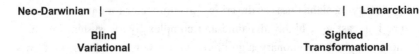

Figure 4 The continuum of evolutionary algorithms. When evolutionary algorithms are placed on a (neo-Darwinian–Lamarckian) continuum, the sightedness dimension (blind-sighted) and the pattern-of-change dimension at the population level (variational-transformational) reduce to one. That is, for any added degree of coupling between variation and selection, the pattern of change, as seen from the population level, becomes ever more transformational in character. Due to the brain producing some coupling between variation and selection, cultural evolutionary algorithms possess *degrees of sightedness*. In the complex matrix of culture, the brain's thought trials can fall anywhere on this continuum, probably exhibiting all degrees of sightedness in-between.

culture as an improved version of essentially the same system. To come right out and say it, my own bias is toward lumping. Here is why. It would be odd if the biospheric version of this mechanism using the most basic of – blind – neo-Darwinian algorithms would not find, sooner or later, a way to improve on itself, to bootstrap so to speak. It did this, apparently, by evolving brains. The partial coupling in creative thinking, the ability to look ahead a few steps, is not only compatible with Darwin's core idea but also an entirely predictable outcome of a system that relentlessly turns the quality crank. It is of such obvious adaptive value that any Darwinian algorithm would eventually hit on a way to evolve better, more sophisticated Darwinian algorithms. And nothing would be more adaptive than making a computational machine – the brain – that is a tad bit less blind.

This same cannot be said about Lamarckian change. Cultural change is not, to turn the argument on its head, a watered-down version of a Lamarckian algorithm. Culture did not come from the 100 percent sighted end of the continuum, from an adaptive guaranteeing instructional process. For the most part, it is not a Lamarckian system with a bit of variation. Given the odd twists and turns and the amount of design waste we see in culture, it would seem more prudent to say that it is a Darwinian system with a bit of sightedness.

We will soon muddle this further. As our novel theoretical framework demonstrates, the mechanism of change operating at any given time in any given cultural problem space can have any degree of sightedness. And, given the weight of the historical baggage attached to these terms, and the fact that actually none accurately describes this complex hybrid system, it might be best to give the mechanisms of change of the system of culture a new name.

3 In the Land of the Blind, the One-Eyed Man Is King

3.1 A Special Class of Prophets?

All parties agree that cultural evolution cannot be reduced to biological evolution. Similar but different seems to be the motto. Except that those who see biological and cultural evolution to be different processes, or at least different enough to warrant discrete treatment, underline the word different, while those stressing that both are members of a common supercategory, with culture being a sort of 2.0 version, underline the word similar. Name the system what you like, we will move on from here.

We have identified the fundamental property that cultural evolutionary algorithms possess that are not part of their biological cousins: Human creating and designing exhibits some coupling of variation to selection. This sightedness, or degrees of sightedness, turns out to be the root cause of all the additional features of the system of culture that cannot be found in nature. Once we accept that human creativity involves cultural evolutionary algorithms with degrees of sightedness generating a mixed variational-transformational pattern of change at the systems level, we can ask more constructive and competent questions.

Specifically, it raises the following, rather obvious, question. How do brains manage to accomplish this partial coupling of variation to selection? Where do the degrees of sightedness come from? Given that we are dealing with, by definition, unknown or novel problem spaces, how do we generate ideational combinations of information that have a higher probability of being adaptive? Unless we are prepared to consider human creators a special class of prophets, we need a sound brain mechanism to explain what otherwise looks like clairvoyance.

In the pages to come, we introduce the prediction paradigm of neuroscience to extract two critical insights. The first is the recent proposal that the brain's predictive computations are the underlying neural mechanism of the sightedness upgrade (Dietrich, 2015; Dietrich & Haider, 2017). The evolutionary treatment of culture gains further traction through the application of prediction processes, because they offer a sound mechanistic explanation at the neurocognitive level for the properties of cultural evolutionary algorithms that set the system of culture apart. The reverse also holds; the relevance of the prediction approach to cultural evolution comes into clear view only when it is framed in terms of a generate-and-test paradigm. Together, they must constitute the bedrock on which to anchor a solid research program on human creativity and cultural evolution.

The second is the idea that prediction is the driving force behind the process of learning. Learning, therefore, can also be understood from a sightedness perspective. This is central for our new theoretical framework that integrates the three kinds of adaptive change of evolution, learning, and development. It is also central to understanding the control system's perspective.

3.2 The Prediction Paradigm

Theorists have been converging from quite different quarters on the idea of prediction as a central purpose of brain function. Predictive processing is a prominent paradigm in neuroscience that presumes that the brain has evolved, fundamentally, to make predictions (Bar, 2007; Grush, 2004; Llinas, 2001; Pezzulo et al., 2008). The claim here is not that the business of anticipating events is one of the brain's important chores, it is *the* main reason for having (big) brains in the first place. It is a perspective that seems counterintuitive at first, but you will warm up to it as soon as you see how it handles otherwise puzzling facts.

The core idea is as follows. We can interact with the world in a nearly infinite number of ways. For behavior to be purposeful and timely in such a high-dimensional setup, the set of possible options must be pruned. We accomplish this by continuously, automatically, and unconsciously generating expectations that meaningfully inform – constrain – perception and action at every turn (Llinas & Roy, 2009; Wolpert et al., 1995). Even when not engaged in a specific task, during stimulus-independent thought, the brain does not idle but actively produces predictions that anticipate future events (Moulton & Kosslyn, 2009). Imagine, for instance, you press the elevator button and there is a delay until you hear the elevator move. You would be immediately surprised, which is only possible if you had an expectation of the future.

That predictive computation is not an optional add-on comes into clear focus when we look at the timescales involved between sensory inputs and motor outputs (Wolpert et al., 1995). Here, we first need to describe the problem to be solved by prediction. The motor system is a distributed, hierarchical set of brain structures that needs an appreciable amount of time to formulate a motor plan and send motor commands down to effector muscles. Sensory systems, for their part, take an equal amount of time for perception. If the interaction between the two is based on *actual* motor execution and *actual* sensory feedback, with one having to await the outcome of the other, the delays would be huge. A sensorimotor cycle that relies solely on such direct engagement, and is limited by real-time neural processing, cannot keep pace with the rate of change between the actor and the environment (Downing, 2009; Grush, 1997). If this were so, life would happen much more slowly than it does (Wolpert et al., 2003).

The motor system solves this timing problem by relying on emulators or predictors that model sensory end states and, based on them, direct upcoming action. As soon as emulation is involved in sensory and motor systems, the processing speed can increase beyond reality-based action and perception (Kawato et al., 1998; Rao & Billard, 1999). This entails that the brain constructs, in addition to simply engaging with the body's inputs and outputs, internal models that simulate the body's inputs and outputs (Grush, 2004). This layer of coding can anticipate the sensory consequences of actions (forward models or predictors) and invoke control processes that guide movement based on known action outcomes (inverse models or controllers) (Bubic et al., 2010; Grush, 2004; Pezzulo et al., 2008). For now, hold that thought, we will come back to it.

3.3 On Learning and Memory

For the challenging task that lies ahead, it is paramount that we briefly go over the standard conception of learning in psychology. What determines conditioning in a Pavlovian paradigm, for instance, is the discrepancy between the occurrence and the predicted occurrence of a reward, the so-called reward-prediction error (Rescorla & Wagner, 1972). Thus, learning depends on the predictability of the reward or, alternatively, the degree of unpredictability (surprise) governs the rate of learning (Schultz, 2000). If the reward-prediction error is positive (more than expected), learning occurs. If the error is negative (less than expected), extinction takes place (Rescorla & Wagner, 1972). Learning ceases when the error falls to zero. It follows from this, somewhat surprisingly, that we do not learn anything at all if we get what we expected, even if repeatedly confronted with the stimulus. Without surprise, there is no change in behavior.

This applies also to reward conditioning, except that in operant learning the difference signal is between expected and actual reinforcement (Downing, 2009). Studies implicate the release of dopamine from neurons in the ventral tegmental area (VTA) in signaling prediction errors. That is, the dopamine signal recognizes discrepancies in expectations. Likewise, dopamine release in the VTA coincides with reinforcement learning, indicating that it processes errors in the prediction of a reward (Schultz, 2000). This places prediction at the heart of associative learning because it stresses the fact that learning occurs as a response to prediction errors (Bar, 2007).

We could define learning, then, as a process that updates emulation errors and optimizes prediction (Wolpert et al., 2003). It is equally correct to say that learning is a process that reduces prediction errors. But for generality, clarity, and the sake of building interdisciplinary bridges, it is essential that we tie this to the evolutionary and engineering terminology we have introduced already.

As such, we could define learning as a process of acquiring controllers. That is to say, learning internalizes the fitness function from the environment to the brain, so that the selection criteria, by virtue of being in the same computational system – the brain – can now be much more tightly coupled to the variation process. This is not possible in biological evolution, where variation occurs in genes and selection in the environment, on the other side of the Weismann barrier. From a sightedness point of view, then, learning is a variation-selection evolutionary algorithm with a very high degree of sightedness, so high in fact that very little, if any, variation occurs. In other words, the directive feedback coming from the controllers make this a no-search, mapping process producing a transformational pattern of change at the population level. But we are getting ahead of ourselves, as the proposal that Lamarckian change, when seen from a sightedness angle, is essentially a learning algorithm is the subject of the next section.

Memory, too, is for prediction. We think of memory as being about the past, while prediction is about the future. The new thinking turns this on its head. Contrary to common sense, the point of memory is not to remember the past but to make information available for simulating the future (Schacter & Addis, 2009). We form memories of the events in our lives to have information available with which to simulate the future (Clark, 2013; Fisher, 2006). If this sounds disturbingly like the sort of talk that would make you edge away if told to you by a stranger on a park bench, think about it in terms of adaptation. What else would memory be for? What good accrues to you by reminiscing about the past? Seen from this perspective, memory is an epistemic device for simulation (Fisher, 2006). Memory is reconstructive and associative, making it essentially the same process as imagination (Bar, 2007; Hassabis & Maguire, 2009; Moulton & Kosslyn, 2009). Memory, in short, serves to enable prediction based on prior experience.

3.4 The Computational Principle

At this point, we need to extract the underlying computational principle of how control systems work. A general and abstract treatment should suffice for our purposes. To get to the bottom of this, we continue with the brain's motor system and how it finds solutions on a known problem space. Take, for instance, how you grab the cup of coffee on the table in front of you, a movement sequence you performed so many times and in so many different ways that your motor system possesses a whole bunch of controllers for it – one for each of the possible action sequences you could execute. We need to lift this computational principle from its home base in motor control, because any lack of clarity here, at the level of *known* problem spaces, is prone to lead to errors in thinking once we apply prediction processes to *unknown* problem spaces – the very essence of the creativity that underlies cultural change.

Predictive mechanisms in the brain challenge the long-held view that information processing is hierarchical and serial. Both paradigms dominating twentieth-century psychology – behaviorism and cognitive psychology – assumed so. The view took for granted that a process starts with the output of a lower-level process and terminates as soon as its output is passed to the next higher stage. The ex post facto variation–selection–inheritance sequence of organic evolution works indeed in that way. However, the pervasiveness of feedforward information flow in cognition shows that this view does not apply to neural processing.

So, back to the cup of coffee in front of you. Neural emulators in the motor system generate an internal model of the required sensorimotor arc to reach this target goal. The internal model has two components: a forward model and an inverse model. They can also be called a predictor and a controller, respectively.

Briefly, and roughly, to model upcoming motion, cortical motor regions generate a motor plan and send a copy of it, the so-called efference copy, to sensory regions in the posterior cortex that co-register the current motor instructions with sensory maps representing the body (Frith, 1992). By virtue of being a copy of the real deal, the efference copy is then used to predict what would happen to your sensory input if you were to grab the cup of coffee as planned. This process is the forward model or predictor of the neural emulator and it converts the motor plan into a representation predicting the sensory consequences of the planned action.

The neural emulator's second component, the inverse model or controller, works the same problem backward. Given the degrees of freedom in a dynamic integration of sensory and motor states, a motor plan cannot specify all possibilities a priori. Plus, as already noted, actual sensory feedback is too slow to inform fluent motor commands. The solution is an inverse model, or controller, that gets hold of the problem from the other end (Diedrichson et al., 2007; Mehta & Schaal, 2002; Wolpert et al., 2003). It asks what motor coordinates you would need to realize the eventual outcome – to grab the coffee mug, that is.

One more step is needed to complete the basic idea. The inverse model controls the process from the back or, if you like, top-down. It generates an efference copy, which goes to the error-predicting forward model to generate a preview of the sensory consequences. By running the efference copy on the brain's sensory maps of the body, error data is generated. That error, estimated by the two components of the neural emulator, is fed once more into the inverse model, updating its motor command, and thus the efference copy, as a result (Wolpert et al., 1995; Wolpert et al., 2003). This optimizing proceeds as the motion unfolds letting both the predictor and the controller converge (for excellent illustrations of these concepts, see Wolpert & Ghahramani, 2000).

You might be relieved to know that this is the stop on the knowledge highway where we can get off. But to make the take-home message vivid and clear, this is a control system in which the desired output is achieved by controlling the input by way of a controller generating a continuously updated actuating signal that is based on error detection. Another way of saying this is that the changing unit's path forward is directed, at every step, by the known adaptive values of the end state – from the top, if you like. The up move, in other words, is highly sighted because the target and the problem space are known.

Unknown problem spaces occur in motor control only if we were to execute a totally new movement – the first time you eat with chopsticks or learn to dance tango, say. (Actually, strictly speaking, these are not instances of unknown problem spaces – they are just unknown to you. An example of an entirely new action sequence at the systems level would be the Fosbury flop, a technique that replaced the scissor move and revolutionized the sport of high jump in the 1970s and 1980s.) Either way, the motor system would not have learned an inverse model for chopstick eating or tango dancing. And without such action memory, the motor system would not even know the algorithm that it needs to solve (Schubotz, 2007; Wolpert, 2003). Lacking this internal paired controller, and therefore prediction error data, the move in this case would have to be gleaned from the environment, by observation or verbal instruction from a teacher.

Just to be clear, seen from a sightedness angle, this example still represents a fully sighted or instructed process of change. The fitness information is accessible, it is just located in the environment. But without its own inverse model, the motor system would produce a very large initial prediction error (which is probably why a first try feels so weird) and thus poor execution. Executing a well-learned motor skill, on the other hand, one that has been practiced a thousand times over, would instead be instructed, or guided, by *internalized* controllers. Learning, in other words, does not change the sightedness parameter of the algorithm. It just moves the location of the controllers, mostly for better performance.

3.5 Bayesian Inference Machines

Learning a motor skill, then, is a control system in which the system's internal operations, or forward steps, are controlled based on a known, adaptive target. The computational principle can also be described by Bayes' theorem. Bayesian statistical inferences is a method to improve a probability estimate as the movement sequence unfolds and additional information becomes available. Any situation requiring a dynamic analysis of a sequence of incoming data can use Bayes' theorem to optimize its approach to a target (e.g., Lau, 2008; Tennenbaum et al., 2011).

The motor system is only one example how we make use of such Bayesian controllers. We also update our beliefs that way when we have to factor in new information. In the words of the motor neuroscientist Daniel Wolpert, we are Bayesian inference machines. In Bayesian language, the predicted motor end state is a prior. A Bayesian prior is a probability distribution that expresses a subjective belief about an event in the future. As new information trickles in, Bayes' theorem calculates the posterior, a probability distribution that takes this new information into account. Put differently, it calculates what effect the new information should have for the prior. The difference between the prior and the posterior is the prediction error that is then used to do one of two things: either the target itself is updated with the posterior becoming the next prior or the target remains the same and the control algorithm is updated.

That this example describes a *known* problem space is important, so it is worth stressing. In a known problem space, the adaptive landscape – controllers, targets, selection criteria, priors, fitness function, and so on – is already known and accessible, at least in principle. Learning the ins and outs of the topography of that known problem space only internalized the controllers – moving them from the environment to the brain. The algorithm of change, however, remains an instructed, or directed, one throughout the learning process. Surely, the acquisition of controllers by the brain matters greatly for the quality of the skilled execution, but we are nevertheless still dealing with a guided process.

Recall that a Lamarckian evolutionary algorithm is a lawful, instructive method of change that has no need for a divine power. This implies that for a Lamarckian process of change to operate, the problem space would have had to be mastered at some earlier point. After all, the instructions cannot come from on high. Keep this in mind, because being clear about this aspect of the mechanism can go a long way to understanding the much more complicated cases of unknown problem spaces in culture. In culture, unknown problem spaces nearly always come with some degrees of sightedness. And the more of a particular problem space is already traversed, by a reigning paradigm say, the better are the brain's predictive computations in generating some visibility of the remaining terrain.

3.6 Hypothetical Controllers

Readers who accept the importance of the brain's prediction competence should have little trouble seeing its profound implications for the creative process and cultural change. Let us explore next how, exactly, the proactive brain generates some sightedness in problem spaces that are *unknown*. The key insight here is the brain's computation of a hypothetical target, a mental representation of the simulated future. This target can then be used to generate a controller. Once this educated guess at a possible solution is in place, neural simulators can exapts the computational principles that first evolved for motor control to take aim at it.

The existence of a predictive goal representation, projected into an otherwise unmapped fitness landscape, is a game changer. It is a hypothetical controller, or in Bayesian language a prior, providing a causal arrow from selection back to variation, resulting in degrees of sightedness. Whatever fitness information it might contain can then direct the occurrence of novel ideas from the top. It does not have to be a full-on hit, any adaptive value greater than zero would do just fine in the long run. In establishing any promising selection criteria, the brain's executive processes – focused attention, working memory, temporal integration, and so on – can configure neural simulators with context, memory, folk wisdom (Colder, 2011; Wolpert et al., 2003), and domain-specific expertise and generate a clever, hypothetical goal representation that can then serve as a fitness function pulling the variation process toward adaptivity.

Now, a Bayesian connecting-the-dots journey can start in earnest. The predictor–controller pair sets up the boundaries of a hypothetical problem space and we can start explorations in terra incognita without being totally blind. Such simulated thought trials ratchet upward in principle in a manner similar – computationally speaking – to those in the motor system. That is, well-established Bayesian revisions could tell us how evolutionary search algorithms converge on creative solutions, even though the topography in that case is unknown. A corresponding mixed variational-transformational pattern of change at the (cultural) population level would show evidence that the variation-selection process has some degree of sightedness.

Think of these hypothetical controllers or priors like a signal flare launched into the dark to get a glimpse of the unfamiliar territory ahead. They provide the means to advance on terrain by focusing on the topography in the distance, rather than on the immediate next step. Suppose the signal flare makes visible a mountain range blocking your way forward. Naturally, you can now eliminate that direction from your journey before trying it.

Now, a whole new computational toolbox is available that the biosphere cannot use, at least not in unknown lands. Of course, we also could always tread into the unknown blindly, letting ourselves be surprised by what might happen – Mother Nature way to proceed. But how much better to have some idea of what might await us. The creative move in this case would be to make a good prediction.

To forestall the ever-present danger of committing the reification fallacy that misconstrues creativity as a single, separate, cohesive, and discrete mental faculty, this computational method is not the only way for creativity to come about. There are also other types of creativity that do not seem to rely on Bayesian hierarchical predictive coding. A blind evolutionary algorithm is one, for instance. But, as we will see soon, a number of other computational methods can generate creative change in the system of culture.

We can also draw out the difference between biological and cultural evolutionary algorithms in terms of heuristics. Being blind, evolutionary algorithms in nature explore problem spaces by running brute, uneducated searches. This kind of exploration contains no speculation as to where in a fitness landscape an up ramp may be located. The evolutionary algorithm relies on brute power and time, not clever short cuts, rendering it neither particularly fast nor efficient. Heuristics, on the other hand, ignore parts of the topography and, in that way, limit the search from the outset (Gigerenzer & Gaissmaier, 2011). With the long shots out of the picture, the evolutionary algorithm can then comb through a more bite size portion of possibilities.

3.7 Cultural Evolutionary Algorithms

Hypothetical controllers give evolutionary algorithms occurring in brains properties that do not exist in the evolutionary algorithm changing nature (Dietrich, 2015). These properties alter the way cultural evolutionary algorithms can move in an unknown problem space, what kind of computational processes they can use, and the type of artifacts they can bring into existence.

First, the sightedness upgrade makes cultural evolutionary algorithms faster and more efficient. It is well known in evolutionary computing that evolutionary algorithms are costly (Eiben & Smith, 2003), especially, of course, a brute force (blind) search. By projecting a potential target that has some fitness information, the search or variation process is more directional, thus reducing the wasteful business of having to explore all possible options. It is probably fair to say that the ability to use heuristics contributes to the much higher rate of change in cultural evolution as compared to biological evolution.

A second property attached to an evolutionary variation-selection algorithm that has a coupling parameter greater than zero is scaffolding. Scaffolding is the temporary support of design features that could otherwise not be part of the final design. Nature does not do future positive effects. It is a shortsighted selection by hindsight. In nature, every variation-selection cycle in a species' trajectory is actualized and must, in its own right, be a viable form. This is because selection occurs after the fact and, importantly, takes place in the real word. The evolutionary algorithm, in other words, cannot jump over impossible intermediates, making the basic move in neo-Darwinian evolution one of generate-and-field-test. Since some designs require elements that cannot be realized without a temporary scaffold, an evolutionary algorithm that requires fitness at every iteration, such as biological evolution, can also not build them. This is true even if suitable mutations were to arise. Not being able to look down the road, not even a single step, nature punishes arriving at the wrong time in the wrong place.

Not so for brains. In brains, selection occurs neither (necessarily) after the fact nor is it (necessarily) located in reality. Brains can short-circuit instantiation and breed multiple generations of ideas in a hypothetical manner. Upgraded like that, the basic move in cultural evolution becomes generate-and-hypothesis-test. Looking ahead in this way, albeit just a few steps, produces a striking effect. Without an instant pay-off requirement, temporarily design elements can be kept in play to figure into subsequent iterations of the evolutionary algorithm. The benefits are higher-order, discontinuous designs that are off limits to biological evolution.

The scaffolding property of cultural evolutionary algorithm is made possible by hypothetical controllers. Comparable to a beacon of light, such a predictive goal representation is a distant target to which to anchor the other side of the scaffold and direct the variation process. Bayesian inference updating can now try to make the ends meet and converge on the creative solution – assuming the imagined controllers have some merit. In that way, we can evolve a thing of beauty even if the intervening steps contain ugly contraptions. An arch is the canonical example of an interlocking design that must leap over nonadaptive, intermediate forms.

A third property of cultural evolutionary algorithms not exhibited by biological ones is foresight or intention. Both are upshots of the sightedness upgrade. By universal agreement, the creative process in the biosphere is not teleological or purposeful. It serves no end, and its designs are neither premeditated nor deliberately initiated in response to a perceived need. That would be evolutionary precognition. Human creators, by contrast, act on purpose; they can have an objective in mind and thus create with intent. The argument from foresight and intention is perhaps the most commonly mooted one to set human creativity apart from creativity in the biosphere and artificial intelligence. In fact, the usually calm waters of academe notwithstanding, people have gone nuts over this point, with some people claiming it to be clear evidence for runaway Darwinism.

But the neural computation of a predictive goal deflates this argument for a categorical difference between cultural and biological evolutionary algorithms, as the experiences of foresight and intention are themselves the computational products of the brain's prediction machinery (Frith, 1992; Wolpert et al., 2003). Refracted through a prediction prism, intention and foresight result from representing the expected future. Like fireworks falling from the sky, hypothetical controllers give the appearance of creative inspiration coming from on high, lest we forget that it was originally shot up there from down below. Foresight and intention, therefore, merely constitute a change to the sightedness parameters of evolutionary algorithms and are thus fully compatible with an evolutionary explanation of the creative process and cultural evolution. This also demonstrates what kind of propulsive force the brain's prediction processes are in explicating the mechanisms underlying human creativity and cultural change.

Finally, the existence of a predictive goal representation allows for entirely different kinds of computational ability is to be used in human creating and designing. Bayesian predictive coding is one, but there are also other computational methods that can now be employed to explore unknown problem spaces, and we will outline them in more detail later on.

4 A Novel Theoretical Framework

4.1 What Would You Say?

Suppose you break into my house in the middle of the night and demand to know the difference between evolution, learning, and development. That would surely make me sit up! To gain some time, I might offer up a few similarities first. Stripped down to the bare generalities, the three processes of evolution, learning, and development can all be understood in the most general sense as gradual, adaptive, and cumulative change. Once I get pressed for the differences, though, I hope the police arrive, because this is much harder than expected.

In recent years, on and off campus, I have put many of my colleagues on the spot asking this question (minus the trespassing). Not surprisingly, just about the only theme I could make out is that the answer depends on the discipline. While biologists might bring up populations, timescales, or inheritance, psychologists would hold forth on Piaget, Darwin, or Skinner. Any hope of distilling even so much as a nuclear definition or some shared terminology among folks from the Departments of Anthropology, Education, or Management has always been dashed at the very latest once computer scientists pitch in, especially those who you would think ought to know – the evolutionary computing or machine-learning types. By the time they are done talking about numerical optimization procedures, search functions, or connection-strengths of nodes in a neural net, I wished I had never asked. The thing that might have kept me sane during this quest is that I have stirred clear of asking this question to the administrators of my university.

On good days, when I am in the mood for even more commotion, I ask a cheeky follow-up question: Given that all three processes cause change, which one is creative? Given the time-tested ability of academics to expand in a vacuum, this brain teaser reliably prompts respectable people, even those of the highest scholarly standing, to rise to levels of speculation that can safely be called imprudent. Everyone, it seems, is an expert on creativity. People are calmly prepared to be educated about plasma physics or computational chemistry, but they think they just know what counts as creative (and what does not), what makes a person creative, and how best to bring it out.

4.2 A Definitional Quagmire

There is a multitude of definitions and meanings attached to the concepts of evolution, learning, and development, even when restricted to a single discipline. The terms are complex, contested, and ambiguous. What's more, just about every discipline has its own terminology, conventions, and traditions on how they should be used and when they apply, none of which carries over to another discipline. So far, no universal definitional characteristic has been identified or even proposed that can unequivocally delineate one process of change from the others.

Of course, within a domain, this definitional quagmire can be addressed to some extent by fiat, which can establish clear boundaries, unique attributes, and a fitting level of analyses for each of these three processes. In biology, for instance, evolution is a change at the population level over generations; learning denotes a change at the individual level during a lifetime; and development is taken to be the process of transforming genotype to phenotype.

But this is a long way from their use in psychology, education, anthropology, computer science, or the R&D (research and development) in industry. For instance, is it language learning or language development? Do corporations develop or evolve? What is the difference between machine learning and evolutionary computing? Is culture an evolutionary or a developmental system? And how does social learning fit into it? Perhaps the greatest challenge to an overarching, discipline-independent understanding of key similarities and differences comes from computer science. In evolutionary computing or machine learning, trials, individuals, timescales, or populations are all fluid concepts (Eiben & Smith, 2003). To take inheritance, neither the conventional coding – genes versus brains – nor the transmission method is applicable, rendering the specifics of heredity, or the substrate, of no use as a marker that could tell evolution from learning. Evolutionary robotics regularly employs deep-learning algorithms, and *genetic* algorithms commonly contain apriori fitness targets (Doncieux et al., 2015) that are actually a component of Lamarckian, but not neo-Darwinian, evolution. Similarly, evolutionary economics uses mathematical models that incorporate evolution and learning into one model (Brenner, 1998), making the model's specifications and dynamics invariant to various inputs, such as different units or populations (Hammond & Axelrod, 2006).

Even within a discipline, when evolution, learning, and development are differentiated by fiat, the definitional quagmire continues with exceptions and violations readily emerging. To stay with biology, evolutionary cycles are generally understood to be long with slower developmental cycles and small mutation rates, so that it takes a long time for changes in the population to manifest themselves. But in some domains, evolution can be very rapid, appearing almost like sudden jumps. To take affinity maturation as an example, the evolutionary processes of the human immune response can occur in a matter of days in just a few generations of B cells (Tonegawa, 1983). Likewise, mutation rates can be very fast indeed, as is the case for various cancers or viruses (Duesberg et al., 2000; Duffy, 2018). Nesting faster learning cycles within longer developmental cycles and still longer evolutionary cycles also proves difficult. The Baldwin effect (Baldwin, 1902) or evo-devo are examples of learning and development not nested within evolution but rather driving it. And this is just a small sample of problems, from one discipline. It appears that the more abstractly one defines evolution, learning, and development, the more recursive the terms become.

In culture, the lines are even more blurred, with additional levels of analysis and interaction effects between evolution, learning, and development multiplying. But to edge us closer to a more comprehensive theory of cultural change, we must identify the core properties of each process and understand how they contribute to the overall composite mechanism of change that drives the system of culture. Pursuing this task promises several rewards. First, it would provide clear leverage to understand the relationship between biological and cultural evolution. Second, it could help shed light on the vexed question of what kind of change might constitute creativity (Dietrich, 2004). And, finally, it can provide a foundation for a more universal theory of change.

4.3 Taking Stock

It is time for a stretch. We brought you a long way to introduce you to a novel theoretical framework that integrates evolution, learning, and development. The proposal does not promise to fix all the tricky definitional problems, but it does present an entirely new angle on how all three mechanisms of change – evolution, learning, and development – related to one another. The new theoretical structure unites them under the single dimension of sightedness, while all other complexities remain temporarily collapsed (units of selection, generational versus individual change, timescales, etc.). Because this exclusive perspective from sightedness uses the mathematical abstraction of algorithms, it can be expressed in terms of control systems and Bayesian coding, making it more independent of discipline. Once secured, we are then in a place from which to see our two barbed issues: what kind of system of change is culture and the pursuit of creativity in that system.

Let us first take stock of where we stand. We started by x-raying the underlying mechanisms of evolution to bring to the fore the key difference between a neo-Darwinian and a Lamarckian evolutionary algorithm. It is the dimension of sightedness! Neo-Darwinian evolution is fully blind, while a Lamarckian system of change is fully sighted. Reduced to a single idea, the difference between them is the coupling of variation to selection, or the accessibility of fitness information. From the viewpoint of the units undergoing the change, a Lamarckian evolutionary algorithm is a process of change in which the selection criteria are accessible or visible. In engineering terms, this is a control system in which controllers provide feedback that then govern the unit's advance.

The other two main dimensions traditionally used to classify evolutionary algorithms can be either collapsed or bracketed. The variational/transformation dimension can be reduced to the sightedness dimension, as the population pattern of change is a function of changes in sightedness. The inheritance dimension can simply be postponed, owing to a rather complete lack of knowledge about the neural code for the representation of knowledge in brains.

Applying this to the system of culture, we can retire the old labels of neo-Darwinian and Lamarckian evolution to culture, because neither describes the overall process of change in culture. Instead, culture and human creativity exhibit degrees of sightedness. Sightedness, then, is the key dimension to understand the character of cultural change.

We then got into the discussion of prediction systems. Leaning heavily on the domain of motor control to work out essential concepts, the exercise provided two critical insights. First, it established a sound mechanistic explanation for the brain's ability to put these few degrees of sightedness into its thought trials. In generating hypothetical controllers, the brain operates cultural evolutionary algorithms with some unique properties, such as faster and more efficient heuristics and the ability to scaffold. Second, it brought into full view that the process of learning can also be subsumed under the sightedness perspective. Learning is a mechanism of change that can be described as a control system. In learning, the changing unit acquires controllers in order to minimize prediction errors and improve performance.

To be crystal clear about it, in learning, change occurs in a principally known problem space. The purpose of predictions in this case is primarily to optimize performance, not to shed light on the unknown. These predictions may affect a particular trajectory to the target, but the target itself is, again, already known in principle. Because the known adaptive selection criteria can serve as anchors to instruct the forward steps of the changing unit, learning or skilled perform-ance can also be phrased in the terminology of Bayesian inferencing.

4.4 Transferring Controllers

This raises the question of where were the controllers before the brain acquired them. The short answer is the environment. This is true for biological evolution as well, of course. The controllers are in the environment. But unlike biological evolution where the Weismann barrier blocks all sight of the adaptive informa-tion, in learning the selection criteria are accessible to the changing unit. In social learning, the information of what is adaptive exists in the shared cultural knowledge of the social environment, either in the brains of other people or as a permanent record.

In language learning, to take one example, the fitness function – the rules of language – is in the linguistic environment and it is clearly communicated, top-down, to the learner. From the learner's point of view, language learning is an instance of a fully sighted control system. This assumes, of course, that infor-mation is not temporarily inaccessible for some reason, which would force the learner into a bit of good-old fashion evolutionary generate-and-test, likely resulting in a case of reinventing the wheel. From the systems (societal) point of view, all units (children) of the system (culture) would change in lockstep, resulting in an overall pattern of change – all children learning their native language – that is transformational. Sure, there is variation among the individual units, but this noise is evolutionarily inconsequential.

What occurs in the process of learning is that the adaptive information is transferred from the social environment to an individual brain. Irrespective of the shared cultural knowledge being in books, digital records, or the brains of parents, it is recruited to instruct the change. Importantly, this transfer does not change the sightedness parameter of the mechanism of change. It remains a control system. Learning simply changes the location of the already accessible fitness criteria. And once the fitness function is internalized and exists in the same computational system – the brain – than the unit doing the changing, behavioral execution is of a totally different quality due to much tighter coupling of predictor–controller pairs and dramatically reduced prediction errors.

Because a Lamarckian control system is not some form of divine creationism (Kronfeldner, 2007), this type of mechanism of change can only be implemented if the problem space is already known at some level 'higher' than the changing unit – the systems level, in other words. Somehow, someone, or something must be able to do the instructing. Naturally, if the problem space is unknown at the systems level, the controllers are inaccessible and thus cannot be made available to provide guiding feedback to the changing units. But once the controllers have been extracted – a known problem space – the change occurring in learning or skilled action is a no-search, mapping process rather than a ratcheting generate-and-test process.

Actually, biological evolution is a mechanism of change that can also be described as the process of acquiring controllers! As said, the controllers in the system of nature are initially located in the natural environment and the transfer here is from the natural environment to a genetic code (epigenetics aside). As the neo-Darwinian algorithm traverses a problem space, in its own blind way of proceeding, the adaptive information is identified and preserved in genes. Another way of saying this is that biological evolution is a process in which the genes acquire controllers.

Importantly, and in stark contrast to the learning mechanism of change, this transfer to genes completely flips the sightedness parameter of the algorithms of change from 0 to 100 percent. This is because evolution converts the problem space it traverses from an unknown to a known one. Learning does not do that; it always occurs in an already known problem space.

Once a problem space in nature is captured and the controllers are saved in genes, the mechanism of change that used to operate as a blind evolutionary algorithm can now be replaced by a more efficient control system that has eliminated the need for a variation-selection process. Put another way, Lamarckian change in nature is simply the fruits of labor of a neo-Darwinian algorithm. One could also say that evolution becomes development once it has done its job. Only when the problem space is mastered at this 'higher level' of genes are the instructions available that can possibly control the output 'from above' in a Lamarckian manner. As for the *next un*known problem space that can now be tackled from the newly attained location in genetic space, the sightedness value of the mechanism of change – evolution – remains zero, always. Anything else would be clairvoyance.

A simple example of a fully mapped problem space is the complex design of an animal's body. The clever solutions to the environmental challenges have been tried and tested over eons of time and built – inherited – as instructions into genes. During the physical development of the individual, the forward steps of the sequence can then unfold – controlled – fully sighted, directed by the internalized, and thus known, controllers coded in the DNA sequence.

In terms of sightedness, the mechanism of change that is development therefore also follows the principles of a control system. It is a no-search, mapping process that relies on established targets. Biology takes development to be the process of transforming genotype to phenotype. In this case, the phenotypical expression of an animal's body – the output – is controlled by the Bauplan coded in genes – the input. And like learning, development is a algorithms of change that can only operate in a known problem space, with a sightedness value that is a Lamarckian, 100 percent from the beginning. But unlike the processes of learning and evolution, the development algorithm does not result in the acquisition or the transfer of any controllers, at least not in nature. They remain in place, on genes, as the developmental mechanism of change does what it does.

4.5 The Framework

We are now in a position to make theoretical hay. It has been argued that no complete understanding of evolution can exist without integrating learning. Plotkin (2011, p. 454), for instance, claims that "if culture is to be causally linked to the processes of evolution, then the first step . . . is understanding the relationship between learning and evolution." Such a relationship is proposed here with our new theoretical framework.

Seen from a sightedness framework, the algorithm describing the Lamarckian process of change and the algorithms describing the processes of change of learning and development can be equated! Accordingly, Lamarckian evolution is a learning or developmental algorithm or, if you prefer, learning or development are examples of a Lamarckian evolutionary algorithm. All three mechanisms of change – Lamarckian, learning, and development – are instances of control systems.

When handling counterintuitive ideas, keeping things lined up properly is good policy. Figure 5, therefore, puts the three mechanisms of change onto a sightedness scale, placing the process of evolution – the blind neo-Darwinian kind – at the zero sightedness end and the two processes of learning and development at the opposite, 100 percent sightedness end. The scale essentially expresses the accessibility of controllers to the changing units.

This sightedness continuum implies a rethinking of what commonly falls under the term evolution. Historically, both Darwinism and Lamarckism have been considered evolutionary processes. This tradition has surely contributed to the failure to integrate evolution with the processes of learning and development into a more comprehensive understanding of change. But according to our new framework, Lamarckian evolution does not count as evolution. It is not an evolutionary algorithm at all, but a learning or developmental algorithm.

This is confirmed, although never quite drawn out this way, by the two most commonly used broad definitions of evolution in biology. The first is the definition used earlier in this Element of a change at the population level over generations, which the Lamarckian algorithm does not produce because its mechanism of inheritance – on phenotypes – does not work in nature. The second is the algorithmic abstraction of evolution popularized by Dawkins (1976) that limits evolution to three conditions: replication, variation, and selection, the latter two of which are not properties of the Lamarckian

Evolution |————————————————————| **Learning and Development**

Neo-Darwinism   Lamarckism
Blind/Variational   Sighted/Transformational

Figure 5 The sightedness continuum: A novel theoretical framework establishing a direct and straightforward relationship integrating evolution, learning, and development along the single dimension of sightedness. This sightedness continuum essentially expresses the accessibility of the fitness function – controllers, targets, priors, selection criteria, and so on – to the units undergoing the change. Based on sightedness, learning and developmental processes are equivalent to the Lamarckian algorithm of change. The fundamental difference to the neo-Darwinian algorithm is the existence of accessible or visible adaptive information. In nature, the process of evolution can be separated from the process of development in a categorical manner. In terms of sightedness, it is all or nothing. In culture however, all three general mechanisms of change mix and mingle, forming a composite mechanism. Due to the brain's prediction system generating hypothetical controllers of some adaptive value, even when the problem space is unknown, the change that takes place at the systems level happens with degrees of sightedness.

algorithm. According to these conventions, and based on our framework, Lamarckian evolution is a misnomer.

But that does not mean that Lamarckism does not exist in nature. It does. As soon as we see Lamarckian "evolution" not as an evolutionary process but a method of change equivalent to development, it is easy to spot it. Nature runs both algorithms of the extreme ends of the sightedness continuum. The neo-Darwinian algorithm operates in unknown problem spaces and the Lamarckian in known problem spaces. Irrespective of how much of a given problem space is already discovered, these two types of problem spaces remain categorically distinct in nature, with their respective mechanisms of change in terms of sightedness included.

Recasting the Lamarckian mechanism of change as a learning or development algorithm requires that we give up on its historical roots, as it was originally conceived of course in the domain of evolutionary theory. But without changing its category, the processes of evolution, learning, and development would remain conflated and a more general framework of change elusive. In putting Lamarckian algorithms into the class of learning or developmental processes, and understanding them in terms of control systems, our new theoretical framework can organize the three mechanisms of change neatly along the single dimension of sightedness.

Anticipating a later discussion of where the three mechanisms of change can be found, our novel framework blurs the lines between the processes of evolution, learning, and development. Not in nature, of course, because here they can still be separated in a categorical manner, located as they are at the extreme ends of the sightedness continuum. But in problem spaces of culture, the change that takes place happens with degrees of sightedness, thanks to the brain's prediction machinery.

It seems, then, that in cultural change, at least as it appears from our framework, the terms of evolution, learning, and development lose their essence. It is all a matter of degrees. In culture, the algorithms of all three mechanisms of change can be involved in change – creative change included. They fuse into a composite mechanism, making it difficult to maintain the identity and definitions that we have traditionally attached to them. What should we do, for instance, with a heuristic algorithm with, say, 50% sightedness? Is it evolution or learning?

4.6 On Learning and Development

Based purely on sightedness, learning and development can be equated. Both are fully sighted control systems, which means that both can only operate when the problem space is already mapped out. But on other grounds, there are differences between these two mechanisms of change. And these differences might come in handy when locating them in nature and culture.

First, there is the matter of controller transfer we were on about earlier. Learning results in the transfer of the adaptive information from shared cultural knowledge to individual brains. For development however, this depends on whether it occurs in nature or culture. In nature, it does not result in the relocation of the fitness function. It remains in place, in genes, as the development mechanism of change advances over time. As we will see shortly, this might be different in culture.

Second, control theory classifies two types of control systems. Depending on the feedback path, these are open loop control systems and closed loop control systems. They map well on to development and learning, respectively.

An open loop control system is a nonfeedback control system in which the output is not fed back to the input. The actuating signal from the controller is not based on error detection and the output has no control over the control action. Rather, the sequence of control action leading to the output is followed regardless of the final results. It is a preprogrammed plan of action that plays itself out without corrective feedback.

The open loop control system describes the mechanism of change that is development. To use an example from nature, phenotypical expression is like running a preset program. A given step of this automatic unfolding does not inform the next step. In the scale of biological organization, there are of course plenty of adjustment processes. At the level of the cellular machinery, for instance, interlocking regulatory feedback loops exist that provide control (Hanahan & Weinberg, 2011). And, as we will see shortly, evo-devo has shown that many developmental processes are not specified in the DNA sequence. To use another example from psychology, dynamic systems theory asserts that human motor and cognitive development is driven by 'multiple, mutual, and continuous interaction of all the levels of the developing system, from the molecular to the cultural' (Thelen & Smith, 2006, p. 258). Thelen and Smith (2006, p. 263) show that the 'dynamic cascade' of human development is the product of patterned interactions between multiple parts that synergistically interact to determine the developmental advance. Without such control processes that adapt the blueprint to the actual local environmental conditions, development would surely be unstable. But for both cases, feedback from the phenotype back to the genotype that supplies the initial input signals would have to cross the Weismann barrier. In that sense, development is a case of an open loop control system.

A closed loop control system is based on feedback in the form of error detection. Here, the controller produces an actuating signal that accepts output information, making the control algorithm a function of the desired outcome. This describes the mechanism of change that is learning with the changing unit being guided toward the adaptive targets by the use of corrective feedback (see Table 1).

Table 1 Summary table of the differences between mechanisms of change

mechanism of change	Sightedness/Feedback	Controller Transfer	Problem Space
Evolution	Blind; no feedback possible	Natural environment to genes	UPS to KPS
Development	Sighted; open loop control system	No controller transfer	Always KPS
Learning	Sighted; closed loop control system	Social environment to brains	Always KPS

Abbreviations: UPS: Unknown problem space; KPS: Known problem space.

Third, the learning mechanism of change actually does not occur in the system of nature! It is only part of culture. Even if, in the process of reading this, you are left shaking your head, undoubtedly thinking of animal learning, please proceed.

Nature only makes use of the two mechanisms of change of evolution and development. While evolution is the process that drives the transfer of adaptive information from the natural environment to genes, development is the process that actuates this genetically coded information. Culture, on the other hand, can use all three. It rarely does so in their pure form however, as it blends them into a composite mechanism of change.

Nature and culture are most commonly distinguished from each other on the basis of the inheritance material. For nature, the substrate is genes; for culture, it is brains. In other words, nature is understood to be a system in which the fitness function is located in either the natural environment or in genes (again, bracketing epigenetics). In contrast, the fitness information in culture is located in the cultural environment, including brains. But not in genes. This difference in the material substance also comes with a fundamentally different coding system for storing information – DNA versus the representational format of the brain which neuroscience has yet to decode.

Learning is a process that occurs only in brains. Genes do not learn. They are neither altered by learning nor is any change in brains due to learning inheritable by genes. This is of course a principal dogma of biology. Organic evolution is Darwinian, not Lamarckian. This goes hand in hand with the understanding that learning is a closed loop control system. In the case of known problem spaces, only brains can use guiding feedback when generating change. Genes cannot accept such guiding feedback. Due to the Weismann barrier, genes are restricted to operating an open loop control mechanism in known problem spaces – development, in other words.

So, what about animal learning, then? Actually, animal learning occupies a curious limbo position in our traditional knowledge framework. On the one hand, the gene–brain division is not contentious. The modern synthesis does not include neural inheritance, it is purely based on genetic transmission. If we accept this partition, we should, as a matter of consequence, accept learning in other animals, given that it occurs in brains, as part of the system of culture. On the other hand, tradition has it that animal learning is part and parcel of the field of biology, and culture is typically restricted to humans. Take for instance Henrich and colleagues' (2008, p. 119) definition of culture again, which captures what is surely the most common conception of culture: "Culture can be understood in the most general sense as information stored in *human* brains" (emphasis added). Animals, then, by definitional fiat, do not have culture. Along with the misclassification of Lamarckism as evolution, leaving animal learning dangling like this has surely contributed to the lack of an integrative framework linking learning and evolution.

It is argued here that it makes little sense to draw the line in the sand on the basis of brain complexity, with human brains producing the realm of culture while less complex brains are relegated to nature. This is a slippery slope at best, if not entirely arbitrary, to say nothing of the palpable anthropocentrism. However, the jump in inheritance substrate from genes to brains marks a fundamental discontinuity, not just in the type of goo but also in the way information is stored, transformed, and inherited. Most importantly, neural networks are able to run predictive computations that generate degrees of sightedness, even if it is just a single degree. Genes cannot run such simulations of the world to generate any sightedness, not even a single degree. So, while the difference in brain complexity between animal species, including humans, is quantitative, a mere matter of degrees, the difference between genes and brains is qualitative.

To follow this line of reasoning all the way to its logical end, one would have to also accept as part of the system of culture animals that do not even have a brain but function on a few thousand neurons forming a basic ganglion chain. Perhaps it is too much to ask to digest the idea of sea slug protoculture, but consequence is consequence.

All this does not preclude the argument that there is a big jump in the artifacts produced by human brains compared to those of other animals. And such an argument would undoubtedly involve the invention of writing or some other way of permanent recordkeeping. If cultural transmission relies on brains only, as it does for other animals, it would always be limited. It is the use of a more stable method of heredity that makes human culture so intensely cumulative. In that sense, it might be fair to argue that cumulative cultural evolution is unique to humans.

4.7 Interaction Effects

There are several complexities we have put on the back burner so far. We are now in a better position to address some of them. The most obvious ones involve interaction effects between the three mechanisms of change. For culture, the processes of evolution, learning, and development blend with each other anyway in unknown problem spaces. The degrees of sightedness resulting from this composite mechanism render any discussion about interaction effects somewhat superfluous. For nature, however, the mechanisms of change remain absolute in terms of sightedness, either zero for unknown problem spaces or total for known problem spaces.

One complexity arising from interaction effects is between biological evolution and learning. In evolutionary biology, this is known as the Baldwin effect. The effect proposes that the general ability to learn can lead to alterations in the genetic composition of a species. Individuals with such a high learning ability adapt faster or better to new environmental challenges, which is an adaptive advantage that can lead to increased reproductive success. The Baldwin effect is considered consistent with the modern synthesis because what is inherited is a general learning ability, which is genetically based and works via natural selection, as opposed to a specific, acquired trait, which would be brain based and therefore Lamarckian. For these reasons, and most importantly, the Baldwin effect does not change the zero sightedness of evolution. In many ways, the Baldwin effect is not different from the general way bigger brains evolve. Those individuals in a population who have slightly bigger brains and, by extension, slightly higher intelligence and learning capability possess an adaptive advantage.

Recall that learning is a mechanism of change that occurs in brains and therefore belongs to the system of culture. But Baldwinian processes are not good examples of nature–culture interactions. This is because it is the general capacity to engage in learning that has an effect on evolution. The learning algorithm itself does not come into play. In true nature–culture interactions, one would expect that the sighted learning algorithm ups the sightedness value of the blind evolutionary algorithm. A better example, therefore, would be the breeding of a particular strain of animals. Another would be if we were to ever engage in large-scale genetic engineering of our own species, with designer babies for instance. These nature–culture interactions clearly increase the sightedness value of biological evolution.

Another complexity arising from interaction effects is between biological evolution and development. Evolutionary developmental biology, or evo-devo, is a field that concerns itself with such interactions. Broadly speaking, it has shown that the complexities of development are more akin to a construction job. Genes do not contain all the detailed information needed for embryonic development. With the genetic blueprint in hand, construction engineers still need to tweak the overall Bauplan – by altering gene expression or gene regulation, for instance – to fit it into the local environment.

Of interest to us here are those developmental processes that are heritable but not encoded in the DNA sequence. There has been quite a bit of sensationalism surrounding this epigenetic inheritance. Some scientists, amplified by an army of Darwin dreaders outside biology, have hyped epigenetics to call for a revolution in biology, but biologists are generally contend to fit epigenetic inheritance within the conceptual framework of the modern synthesis. In the end, it should not be too surprising that an evolutionary algorithm that ratchets upwards finds, sooner or later, some other material to preserve useful (adaptive) information (the brain is the ultimate example of that). Epigenetics *looks* Lamarckian but it is not. Epigenetic changes are under the control of natural selection and do not change the sightedness value of biological evolution.

5 Places of Change
5.1 The View from the Changing Unit

The trail we have taken so far has brought into full view what types of mechanisms of change exist and how they work. Having clarified their ways of generating change and how they relate to one another, it is now time for an examination of where they can be found and when they come into play. Using our theoretical framework as a viewing platform, we have already caught glimpses of this here and there, both in nature and in culture, but a more systematic survey is now needed because any lack of clarity here is prone to lead to pointless objections once we push further up the trail to see our two barbed issues: what kind of system of change is culture and what kind of change in that system counts as creativity.

For this task, we must distinguish for both systems of change, nature and culture, problem spaces in which the topography is known, at least in principle, from those in which it is basically unknown. This yields a 2×2 matrix – system of change (nature versus culture) and problem space (known versus unknown). Thinking through this structured space is a disciplined and vigorous exercise that we embark on next.

Based on our sightedness framework, known and unknown problem spaces can be understood in the most general sense in terms of the changing unit's access to the selection criteria. Taking this perspective of the changing – evolving, learning, or developing – unit, we ask what it can know about these fitness criteria. Of course, 'knowing' here is not meant in an anthropomorphic sense but is simply a way to indicate the visibility or sightedness the changing unit might have of the fitness function, which, in turn, determines the type of algorithms of change it can use to advance in the problem space.

Changing units face an unknown problem space when they have no knowledge of the criteria determining adaptivity. Given this zero visibility, changing units in nature must run a neo-Darwinian algorithm to find out about it. The resulting blind, trial-and-error process produces, at the systems level (all individual units taken together), a variational pattern of change. Changing units in culture, on the other hand, can generate hypothetical knowledge of the fitness function, and, with this bit of foresight, the pattern of change at the systems level becomes a mixed one.

Changing units face a known problem space when they have knowledge of the criteria determining adaptivity. A known problem space naturally includes unknown parts because coverage of a topography is rarely total. But as long as the big peak of the topography is scaled, and we know the general layout and basic regularities of the landscape, the problem space can be counted as known in principle. This might leave plenty of unvisited local maxima still to be found. And although these lesser peaks represent, strictly speaking, virgin territory, these novel spots need not have been previously stepped on before we can benefit from a control algorithm, as they obey the same underlying regularities. An algorithm exploring these unknown gaps of in-principle known spaces would be highly sighted. Indeed, our brain's neural simulators could be fed with so much information about them that the actual search algorithm might not need a variation-selection component at all, although we are dealing with hitherto unseen places.

In known problem spaces, trial-and-error becomes (largely) unnecessary, and the changing units can guide their own changing process by utilizing the computational toolbox that comes with control systems. This access to the problem space's fitness function produces, at the systems level, a transformational pattern of change, because all individual units of the system change together in the same direction of good.

Consider, for instance, the invention of the periodic table by Dmitri Mendeleev in the 1860s. This new organization of the then known chemical elements – the big peak – represented a new paradigm in chemistry that made the discovery of yet unknown elements – the local maxima – highly sighted, since now scientists knew what exactly to look for. The subsequent discovery of radium and polonium by Marie Curie around the turn of the century was the outcome of a very foresightful, systematic search strategy. Few people were surprised by the eventual discovery. But few people would also be prepared to argue that this does not count as creativity.

We could say then that problem spaces in culture are not clear-cut. Unknown problem spaces are rarely, if ever, totally unknown, and known problem spaces are often not totally known. As such, there are opportunities for creativity in both. But this is not to say that the properties of their mechanism of change are not different.

5.2 A Systematic Survey

Figure 6 is a 2×2 diagram plotting, for each of the four cases, the location of the fitness function, the type of mechanism of change in operation, and the overall

Problem Space (PS) at Systems Level

Known PS   Unknown PS

	Known PS	Unknown PS
Nature	Development FF: Genes MC: open loop control system Pattern: Transformational	Biological Evolution FF: Natural Environment MC: Neo-Darwinian EA Pattern: Variational
Culture	Learning / Development FF: Environment / own brain MC: control system Pattern: Transformational	Cultural Change FF: Environment / own brain MC: Degrees of sightedness Pattern: Mixed

Systems

Figure 6 A summary diagram of the mechanisms of change based on sightedness. For details, see the corresponding text. Abbreviations: FF: fitness function; MC: mechanism of change; PS: problem space; EA: evolutionary algorithm.

pattern of change evident at the systems level. Keep in mind the exclusive perspective of sightedness we adopt in our framework that holds all other dynamics that might exist between the mechanisms of change temporarily collapsed – generational versus individual change, inheritance mechanism, units of selection, timescales, storage format, and so on. The three mechanisms of change – evolution, learning, and development – are reduced to the sightedness variable and plotted as a function of the system of change (nature versus culture) and problem space (known versus unknown).

We start with the system of nature. We first work out the unknown problem spaces (upper-right quadrant) followed by the known problem spaces (upper-left quadrant). Continuing in a counterclockwise direction, we move to the system of culture and consider first the known problem spaces (lower-left quadrant). One might be forgiven for thinking that there is no place for creativity here but, as we will see, this is not so. This, then, sets us up for the special case of culture and unknown – or rather partially known – problem spaces (lower right quadrant). Naturally, we also look for creativity in this region of interest.

5.3 Problem Spaces in Nature

An unknown problem space in nature is the standard case of evolutionary biology. And of course, it is the domain of the neo-Darwinian evolutionary algorithm. In this territory, the fitness function is located in the natural environment and the changing unit has no knowledge of it. This inaccessibility of the adaptive landscape due to, one, the Weismann barrier and, two, the system's total lack of prediction abilities to simulate possible targets means that the neo-Darwinian evolutionary algorithm must explore this new terrain blind. The Lamarckian, 100 percent sighted algorithm is impossible here. Indeed, with zero degrees of sightedness, all the computational tools of a control system are off limits.

A known problem space in nature is the result of the neo-Darwinian algorithm doing its thing. As it roams a problem space, the selection criteria are identified, and the biological inheritance mechanism preserves the hard-won information in genes (again, bracketing epigenetics). This conquest transfers the location of the fitness function from the natural environment to genes, inside the very unit undergoing the change. And once the controllers are coded in the DNA sequence, the terrain is a known problem space for the changing unit. This is the domain of the development mechanism of change – an open loop control system, to be precise – in which the changing unit is transformed based on a preprogrammed sequence of commands, at least in its broad strokes. Again, such a control system can possibly only be implemented if the targets are known at some level higher than the changing unit, which in this case are the controllers located in genes.

"Evolutionary processes are themselves evolutionary products" (Godfrey-Smith, 2007, p. 210). In nature, the Lamarckian or development method of change is simply the product of the process of evolution. Here, then, is another way to express the relationship between them: Evolution becomes development once the adaptive peaks of the fitness landscape are acquired. During accumulate adaptive change, the blind evolutionary algorithm presses ahead into unknown territory, while the already conquered territory – the accumulated bit – is left to a much faster and more efficient – meaning sighted – mechanism of change.

Yet another way of putting this is that, in nature, evolution converts unknown problem spaces into known ones so that development can take over. From a computational or functionalist point of view, this is what makes change accumulate in the first place. Inheritance can be seen as the implementation of a much faster and more sophisticated mechanism of change, one that is on the opposite end of the sightedness spectrum and, because of that, does away with the slow and wasteful business of variation and selection. The territory that is novel for the changing unit (but not novel at the systems level) can now be recrossed in short order, with very few errors.

Since phenotypical changes resulting from learning and development are not inheritable in nature, and since nature does not possess prediction capabilities the way the system of culture does with brains, known and unknown problem spaces, along with their respective mechanisms of change, are distinct categories. In nature, no algorithms of change exists that possesses sightedness in degrees. Sightedness is either zero or total. And the sightedness parameter also does not change as a function of advances in a given problem space.

5.4 Known Problem Spaces in Culture

Known problem spaces in culture have additional complexities that do not exist in nature – prediction processes, most importantly. But even with the inevitable unknown gaps that exist in any in-principle known topography included, known problem spaces are no different in terms of sightedness to those in nature. We constantly master domains by extracting their critical utility values and keep the acquired knowledge someplace – books, digital records, other brains, and so on. The accumulated knowledge can then be told, or shown, to individual changing units and they do not have to trial-and-error to find out what might constitute an up ramp in the topography. This is the domain of the learning or development – or Lamarckian – algorithm in which the arrow of causation runs top-down, and the overall pattern of change of the system is transformational.

In culture's known problem spaces, the location of the fitness information is in the social environment. Such shared cultural knowledge is then used to guide the learning or developing unit in the desired direction. Consider again language acquisition, but this time in the context of open and closed control systems. We have already posted the question of whether language acquisition is a case of learning or development. The acquisition of a native language seems to better fit the label of development, as the process has elements of an open loop control system. There is the sense that a program is unfolding, a preset sequence of steps, that is helped along by the mere exposure to target information. The acquisition of a second language in adulthood, however, seems to better fit the label of learning. As any adult who tried it can tell you, not much will unfold automatically by just being exposed to the linguistic environment. It is all about top-down, corrective feedback. This is not a clear-cut separation, of course, which just reinforces the fact that change, in culture, is the result of a blend of the mechanisms of change.

What the processes of learning and development in culture accomplish is to relocate the controllers from the social realm to individual brains. Again, this act does not alter sightedness, as the fitness information is already known at the systems level. The mechanisms of change of learning and development, in other words, start and end sighted. They are control systems throughout. But by internalizing the knowledge, something else is accomplished. Individuals now possess their own (neural) representation, which greatly enhances the quality of the output.

And this brings us back to prediction. Nature does not do prediction, not in known problem spaces and certainly not in unknown problem spaces. Even in its sighted operations, nature only supports the development mechanisms of change, which is an open loop control system that cannot incorporate feedback. Nature, therefore, cannot benefit from prediction at all. Of course, the brain uses predictive computations in both problem spaces. In unknown problem spaces, prediction boosts the creative process. In known problem spaces, however, it has two functions. First, it also boosts the creative process. But before we get to that, let us first look at the other function: boosting of performance.

Take the straightforward example of learning a motor skill – say, playing tennis. In learning, the brain establishes specialized predictor–controller pairs so that for all possible forward moves or predictors, there are principally known consequences or controllers. This internalizing dramatically lowers prediction errors, and with less error variability, action sequences can become speedier and more accurate.

Now, consider the application of what was learned – say, the performance of an experienced tennis player. Once an individual brain possesses a neural representation of the controllers, we are no longer dealing with learning but with behavioral execution. If learning is the acquisition of controllers, skilled performance is the use of them. The difference between them does not lie in the sightedness value of the mechanism of change. In both cases, the change occurs in known problem spaces, and both are fully sighted control mechanisms. It lies in the effect the expert performance has on the environment. Interestingly, unlike the study of learning, the field of motor control readily uses the principle and terminology of control engineering to describe its phenomena.

Let us take another example of predictive coding in known problem spaces that also does not count as creativity and that does not depend on movement – imagining the future. The planning out one's morning chores or the game of chess are cases in point. The controllers as well as the algorithms that need to be solved are principally known. Because of that, we can calculate the outcomes of several steps in advance before making a move. The brain runs simulation chains that reason through a series of choice points in the future. For all possible forward moves, there are principally known consequences. Accounting for the fact that the future is never certain, there is total sightedness of the fitness landscape. It is essentially a mapping process in which the forward steps are coupled to their known adaptive values. These are examples of strategic thinking and clever decision-making, but not examples of discovery and creativity.

But there are opportunities for discovery and creativity in principally known problem spaces. The key to understanding this is, again, the brain's prediction system. One might be forgiven for thinking that creativity in known problem spaces sounds like a contradiction but recall that many problem spaces are not charted in all their exhaustive detail. Often there are gaps, perhaps even significant gaps. Another way of putting this is in terms of treads of actuality. Think of a logical space that contains all possible permutations of information. All creations, every design that has been made and every design that could be made, complex or simple, actual or potential, biological or cultural, alive or artificial, have their proper place somewhere within it. Any thread of actuality that emerges from this vastly larger set of possibilities has adjacent trajectories that are not being actualized. We can think of the size of these uncharted gaps in an otherwise known problem space as the distance between threats of actuality.

It is a popular but misbegotten tradition to dismiss this type of creativity as mere problem-solving or logical reasoning. Our overly romantic and mystified view of creativity prevents us from appreciating that creative acts need not be wild, or even surprising, to count as creativity. Anything or anyone making upward moves in unknown regions of the logical space of possibilities can be said to create and design.

5.5 Unknown Problem Spaces in Culture

In theory, an unknown problem space in culture is fully uncharted territory at the systems level. No one has ever set foot in there. Not even the underlying regularities of the fitness landscape have been explicated. Any foray into this space surely counts as creativity.

After many millions of years of biological evolution and many millennia of cumulative cultural evolution, human creators today rarely face such totally unknown problem spaces, however. First, brains have extracted good design principles – folk physics, folk psychology, linear logic, and so on – from the common stock of design elements, and since these common solutions to common problems yield a bit of sightedness, they have accumulated over time, becoming integrated into the neural hardware as a result (Dennett, 1995; Pinker, 2002). Our brains come with a whole stack of these cognitive tools preloaded and preinstalled that can inform – give direction to – the search process. But as excellent as this array of hardwired pruning techniques is, what really boosts the sightedness value of the mechanism of change by orders of magnitude is the brain's prediction machinery. The human mind is such a heavy lifter in the creativity department because our neural simulators can use culture's accumulated wealth of knowledge to generate predictive representations of the world that informs the generate-and-test algorithms roaming terra incognita. In other words, unlike in nature, in culture, the already-known parts can help out with discovering the still unknown parts.

For these reasons, it seems unlikely that the neo-Darwinian evolutionary algorithm, in its pure, totally blind form, exists in culture. Something can always be gleaned before stepping into the unknown. Perhaps the closest, recent example of a rather unknown problem space was the directionless phase in the beginning of quantum physics in 1900. The negative result of the famous Michelson–Morley experiment, a study that provided conclusive experimental proof that there was no luminiferous ether, effectively put an end to the Newtonian paradigm, leaving physicists temporarily with no alternative. The new quantum realm was, and still often is today, so alien to the brain's prediction capabilities that the mechanism of change in the early days of the quantum paradigm was probably very close to the blind end of the sightedness scale. Not anymore. The more mature a paradigm gets, the more powerful become our prediction abilities. The brain gives unknown problem spaces in culture aspects of control systems.

The degrees of sightedness upgrade to the blind, neo-Darwinian evolutionary algorithm makes cultural evolutionary algorithms much faster and more efficient explorers of an unknown topography. In addition, hypothetical controllers bring cognitive scaffolding into play with which we can create completely different classes of artifacts not possible in nature.

There is no good, overall name for the mixed dynamic of change in culture's unknown problem spaces. So far, our knowledge catalogue has recognized and labeled only the categories at both extreme ends of the sightedness continuum. But, strictly speaking, a composite mechanism that possesses the property of sightedness in degrees is not evolution; it is not learning; it is not development; and it is not a control system. It also cannot be designated neo-Darwinian or Lamarckian and the overall pattern of change does not fit the classes of variational or transformational. What's more, we will see shortly that the actual degree of the composite mechanism's sightedness is also a moving target.

5.6 Creative Change in Culture

The novel theoretical framework presented here organizes the three different mechanisms of change based on sightedness. By fleshing out how they work in terms of the sightedness property, we could undertake a systematic analysis of problem spaces in nature and culture to see how, where, and when they cause change to happen. With this in hand, we are now in a position to reexamine our two barbed issues: what kind of system of change is culture and what in that system counts as creative change. We have already touched on creativity in many places, but there are additional considerations, especially given that problem spaces in culture are not clear-cut. Unknown problem spaces contain known, even if only hypothetically known, parts and known spaces contain unknown parts. Creativity, therefore, can be found in both. But this is not to say that there are not any differences.

There has been a long tradition to distinguish the kind of creativity that is often described as problem-solving, systematic, analytical, effortful, or even dull from the often celebrated kind of creativity that is wild, spontaneous, unconscious, effortlessness, accidental, or even crazy. Sure enough, from Kekulé's daydream of whirling snakes forming a (benzene) ring to Newton watching apples fall (a myth likely originating from Voltaire), Coleridge's conception of the poem Kublai Khan, and Archimedes displacing bathwater, such flashes of insight are the very cliché of the creative genius.

This tradition has often gone so far, both in popular culture and academia, as to regard only the latter as *true* creativity and take the former to be either inferior or to dismiss it altogether. If so, what are we going to do with Marie Curie? And, what would we make of Edison's "empirical dragnet" method that yielded a total of 1,093 patents; Watson and Crick's methodical approach of testing the stability of DNA base pairs; the clever ways in which NASA engineers solved the problems of the otherwise doomed Apollo 13 mission; or the countless occasions we converge on creative solutions by logically, analytically, systematically, and deliberately reasoning through a given problem space.

Certainly, both types cause change that is novel or original. In fact, both conform to the most widespread definition of creativity, something that is novel and useful. For our present purposes, we can steer clear of characterizing creativity beyond the standard definition, perhaps with the caveat that any additional criteria for creativity would only apply to certain types of creativity (Dietrich, 2019). As such, anything or anyone making up moves in an unknown topography can be considered to create and design.

Novel, unknown problem spaces in culture are difficult terrain. Just finding them is difficult, never mind solving them. Often, we do not even know they exist, like the quantum world before 1900. And if we do, if the big peak of the space has not been conquered, and we have next to no understanding of the structure and pattern of the landscape or its basic underlying regularities, our prediction system is of little help. A field of science that lacks an overarching paradigm is a good example. Neuroscience, for instance, does not have an equivalent to what are the organizing summits of biology's topography, the theory of evolution or the principles of genetics. We have no grand theory of brain function the way chemistry does with the periodic table or physics with the theory of relativity and the standard model. The field of consciousness is in the same place. No one knows how a comprehensive paradigm might even look like.

But once the major peak is scaled and a reigning paradigm is in place, work can begin on mapping the minor peaks and filling the gaps in-between. For the early excursions into the still unknown parts, sightedness is likely to be low. However, from the grand view of the major peak, the brain's subsequent creative trips into the surrounds have ever more degrees of sightedness. As we explicate more and more controllers, our neural simulators can use them to make ever more accurate predictions. By the late stages of a paradigm, the sightedness of the mechanism of change is likely to be high. And with any added degree of coupling of variation to selection in the algorithms of change the overall pattern of change exhibited by the paradigm during its lifetime would go from variational to transformational. In the end, a mastered paradigm – Newtonian physics, for instance – can be taught in schools. It falls under the learning mechanism of change.

At what point we can consider a problem space to be known in principle is obviously open to debate, although scaling the big peak is a rather large step toward control system operations. Clearly, unknown and known problem spaces are on a continuum; and so is creativity. It is useful however, as we have done, to distinguish problem spaces so that we can better work out their key features. And, not to forget, in nature they are actually categorically separate classes.

From this we can deduce that there is a reciprocal causal interaction between sightedness, knowledge, and prediction. The degree of sightedness is a function of accumulated knowledge and prediction capabilities. Specifically, the more is known about the problem space, the better can the still unknown parts be predicted, the higher becomes the sightedness value of the mechanism of change which, in turn, leads to an even faster accumulation of knowledge of the problem space. The creative process, in other words, changes the mechanism of change of the creative process itself. The sightedness parameter turns out to be a moving target. In the beginning of exploring a certain problem space, the algorithm's central feature is a variation-selection process; in the end, its central features are control system operations.

5.7 The System of Culture

So, what then can we say about the nature of the system of culture? Given our novel sightedness framework and our analysis of how, where, and when the mechanisms of change cause change to happen, what conclusions can we draw about the overall character of culture? One thing is certain, a complex picture has emerged.

One straightforward conclusion is that a mechanism of change that has partial sightedness defies classification. The mechanism is not evolution – the blind, neo-Darwinian kind – and it is not a control system – neither the Lamarckian nor the learning or development kind. Perhaps the mechanism causing cultural change should get its own name, as it is a composite in terms of sightedness, a blended mix of the three mechanisms. This is particularly true for creative change.

A second conclusion is that the composite mechanism itself changes. The sightedness value is in constant flux, changing as a function of advances in a given problem space. The system of culture, therefore, is not powered by an underlying mechanism that is fixed to one parameter on the blind-sighted or variational-transformational dimensions. This is not the case for nature, of course, where this value is permanently fixed to one parameter – zero – irrespective of what effect the mechanism has on the system. In culture, the sightedness value not only differs from domain to domain but also changes within a domain over time as a function of available knowledge and prediction capability. From this reciprocal causal interaction between sightedness, knowledge, and prediction, we can state that the brain's creative thought trials not only generate cultural artifacts but, in the course of doing so, also change the very character of the mechanism causing the creative change itself. It all makes for a very noisy signal in the overall pattern of change of the system.

Before we get to a third conclusion about the system of culture, there is an additional layer of complexity that deserves special mention. One, because this conclusion seems irreconcilable with a Darwinian account of culture and, two, because it still cannot be used to push for a Lamarckian label. It involves mechanisms of change in *unknown* problem spaces that contain no variation and no selection processes whatsoever. To be clear, we are here talking about a 100-percent sighted algorithms of change operating successfully in virgin territory or, if you like, creativity with no trial-and-error component at all.

Examples include backtracking algorithms, recursive algorithms, divide-and-conquer algorithms, or deep-learning algorithms such as the recent large language generative AI models. Computer scientists use these techniques all the time to find new solutions and there is nothing to suggest that we do not use them, or aspects of them, for our own creative explorations as well. Some of these complex algorithms have preset targets baked into them that can guide their advance, while others just unfold like an open loop control system. They are then let loose in a virgin corner of the topography. The outcome might well be novel and useful.

Alternatively, the trajectory followed by the sequence of computational steps might produce something creative. Think of a painting or a piece of music. They result from the performance of a learned skill. Any one step of the painting process is not novel by itself. Each step is executed based on internalized controllers. But the sequence of steps generates an image that might be deemed creative. AI's large language models that are based on deep-learning algorithms are generative that way. During the learning process, the network structure implanted controller information in their nodes and strength of connections. Using this configuration, the AI then generates text without any variation-selection element in place.

Such an approach to creativity is often preferable. Computationally speaking, evolutionary algorithms are expensive with their need to explore many alternatives (Doncieux et al., 2015), and once a task is basically understood, there is always a more specific and efficient algorithm to make progress than an evolutionary algorithm (Eiben & Smith, 2003). But although these algorithms do not work with an evolutionary ratchet, they are still the outcome of one. Recall that "evolutionary processes are themselves evolutionary products" (Godfrey-Smith, 2007, p. 210). And that is the reason why these strategies cannot serve to push for a Lamarckian label. The existence of a cumulative design in the system – a control or Lamarckian algorithm, in this case – is no grounds for the claim that culture is not an evolutionary system. Such an argument would be broadly analogous to the statement that the existence of a cumulative biological design – an animal's body, for instance – is evidence that nature is not an evolutionary system. The effects of such control algorithms on mathematical models of cultural change have often led to the false conclusion that culture is not Darwinian.

A third conclusion is that all this complexity at the mechanism level generates a noisy and ever-shifting dynamic of change at the system level. The system overall, therefore, also defies classification. It is not (neo)Darwinian and it is not Lamarckian. The pattern of change as a whole is not variational and it is not transformational. In short, culture is its own thing. Although there are still plenty of people holding on to a view of either extreme, this conclusion is not exactly breaking news for the majority in the field. But this Element has provided new insight into the how and why.

Perhaps the system of culture should get its own name, matching the new one for its underlying mechanism. As already said, its predominant designation as an evolutionary system depends primarily on whether you are a lumper or a splitter. One could legitimately ask, for instance, how many degrees of sightedness should be involved in creative change before we could label the whole system, say, cultural development instead of cultural evolution? Perhaps the term cultural evolution is still preferable to describe the system as a whole, because the root cause of all this complexity – the brain – is, after all, itself a product of evolution. And perhaps the term cultural evolution is also still preferable, because we might not have as many degrees of sightedness in our thought trials as we think we have.

References

Baldwin, J. M. (1886). A new factor in evolution. American Nature, 30, 441–451.

Baldwin, J. M. (1902). Development and evolution. New York: Macmillan.

Bar, M. (2007). The proactive brain: Using analogies and associations to generate predictions. *Trends in Cognitive Science*, 11, 280–289.

Bar, M. (2009). The proactive brain: Memory for prediction. Philosophical Transactions of the Royal Society B, 364, 1235–1243.

Barsalou, L. W. (2009). Simulation, situated conceptualization, and prediction. Philosophical Transactions of the Royal Society B: Biological Sciences, 364, 1281–1289.

Boyd, R., & Richerson, P. J. (1985). Culture and the evolutionary process. Chicago: University of Chicago Press.

Brenner, T. (1998). Can evolutionary algorithms describe learning processes? Journal of Evolutionary Economics and Evolution, 8, 271–283.

Brown, G. R., Dickins, T., Sear, R., & Laland, K. N. (2011). Evolutionary accounts of human behavioural diversity. Philosophical Transactions of the Royal Society Series B, 366, 313–324.

Bubic, A., Von Cramon, D. Y., & Schubotz, R. I. (2010). Prediction, cognition and the brain. Frontiers in Human Neuroscience, 4. doi:10.3389/fnhum.2010.00025.

Burke, J. (1995). Connections. New York: Little Brown & Co. Press.

Campbell, D. T. (1960). Blind variation and selective retention in creative thought as in other knowledge processes. Psychological Review, 67, 380–400.

Clark, A. (2013). Whatever next? Predictive brains, situated agents, and the future of cognitive science. Behavioral and Brain Sciences, 36, 1–73. doi:10.1017/S0140525X12000477.

Colder, B. (2011). Emulation as an integrating principle for cognition. Frontiers in Human Neuroscience, 5, 1–12. doi:10.3389/fnhum.2011.00054.

Darwin, C. (1859/1968). *The origin of species*. London: Penguin.

Dawkins, R. (1976). The selfish gene. Oxford: Oxford University Press.

Dawkins, R. (1986). The blind watchmaker. New York: W.W. Norton.

Dennett, D. C. (1995). Darwin's' dangerous idea. New York: Simon & Schuster.

Diedrichsen, J., Verstynen, T., Hon, A., Zhang, Y., & Ivry, R. B. (2007). Illusions of force perception: The role of sensori-motor predictions, visual information, and motor errors. Journal of Neurophysiology, 97, 3305–3313.

Dietrich, A. (2004). The cognitive neuroscience of creativity. Psychonomic Bulletin & Review, 11, 1011–1026.

Dietrich, A. (2007). Introduction to consciousness. London: Palgrave Macmillan.

Dietrich, A. (2015). How creativity happens in the brain. London: Palgrave Macmillan.

Dietrich, A. (2019). Types of creativity. Psychonomic Bulletin and Review, 26, 1–12.

Dietrich, A., & Haider, H. (2015). Human creativity, evolutionary algorithms, and predictive representations: The mechanics of thought trials. Psychonomic Bulletin & Review, 22, 897–915.

Dietrich, A., & Haider, H. (2017). A neurocognitive framework for human creative thought. Frontiers in Psychology: Cognitive Science, 7, 2078–2085.

Dietrich, A., & Kanso, R. (2010). A review of EEG, ERP and neuroimaging studies of creativity and insight. Psychological Bulletin, 136, 822–848.

Doncieux, S., Bredeche, N., Mouret, J., & Eiben, E. A. (2015). Evolutionary robotics: What, why, and where to. Frontiers in Robotics AI, 2, 1–18.

Downing, K. L. (2009). Predictive models in the brain. Connection Science, 21, 39–74.

Duesberg, R., Stindl, R., & Hehlmann, R. (2000). Explaining the high mutation rates of cancer cells to drug and multidrug resistance by chromosome reassortments that are catalyzed by aneuploidy. Proceedings of the National Academy of Sciences, 97(26), 14295–14300.

Duffy. S. (2018). Why are RNA virus mutation rates so damn high? PLoS Biology, 16, e3000003.

Eiben, A. E., & Smith, J. E. (2003). Introduction to evolutionary computing. New York: Springer.

Fisher, R. A. (1930). The genetical theory of natural selection. Oxford: Oxford University Press.

Fisher, J. C. (2006). Does simulation theory really involve simulation? Philosophical Psychology, 19, 417–432. doi:10.1080/09515080600726377.

Frith, C. D. (1992). The cognitive neuropsychology of schizophrenia. Hove: Lawrence Erlbaum.

Gigerenzer, G., & Gaissmaier, W. (2011). Heuristic decision making. Annual Review of Psychology, 62, 451–482. doi: 10.1146/annurev-psych-120709-145346.

Godfrey-Smith, P. (2007). Conditions for evolution by natural selection. Journal of Philosophy, 104, 489–516.

Gould, S. J. (1979). Shades of Lamarck. Natural History, 88, 22–28.

Grush, R. (1997). The architecture of representation. Philosophical Psychology, 10, 5–23.

Grush, R. (2004). The emulation theory of representation: Motor control, imagery, and perception. Behavioral and Brain Sciences, 27, 377–396.

Hammond, R., & Axelrod, R. (2006). The evolution of ethnocentrism. Journal of Conflict Resolution, 50, 926–936.

Hanahan, D., & Weinberg, R. A. (2011). Hallmarks of cancer: The next generation. Cell, 144, 646–674.

Hassabis, D., & Maguire, E. A. (2009). The construction system of the brain. Philosophical Transactions of the Royal Society B: Biological Sciences, 364, 1263–1271. doi:10.1098/rstb.2008.0296.

Henrich, J., Boyd, R., & Richerson, P. J. (2008). Five misunderstandings about cultural evolution. Human Nature, 19, 119–137.

Huxley, J. (1942). Evolution: The modern synthesis. London: Allen & Unwin.

Jablonka, E., & Lamb, M. J. (2014). Evolution in four dimensions: Genetic, epigenetic, behavioral, and symbolic variation in the history of life. Cambridge, MA: MIT Press.

Kawato, M., Kawato, M., & Wolpert, D. (1998). Internal models for motor control. Sensory Guidance of Movement, 218, 291–307. doi: 10.1016/S0959-4388(99)00028-8

Kronfeldner, M. E. (2007). Is cultural evolution Lamarckian? Biology and Philosophy, 22, 493–512.

Kronfeldner, M. E. (2010). Darwinian "blind" hypothesis formation revisited. Synthese, 175, 193–218.

Lau, H. (2008). A higher order Bayesian decision theory of consciousness. In R. Banerjee, & B. K. Chakrabarti (Eds.), Models of brain and mind: Physical, computational, and psychological approaches (pp. 37–48). Boston: Elsevier.

Lewontin, R. C. (1970). The units of selection. Annual Review of Ecology and Systematics, 1, 1–18.

Lewontin, R. C. (1991). Biology as ideology. New York: Harper.

Llinás, R. R. (2001). I of the vortex: From neurons to self. Boston: MIT Press.

Llinás, R. R., & Roy, S. (2009). The "prediction imperative" as the basis for self-awareness. Philosophical Transactions of the Royal Society B, 364, 1301–1307.

Mayr, E. (1981). The growth of biological thought: Diversity, evolution and inheritance. Cambridge, MA: Harvard University Press.

Medawar, P. M. (1953). A commentary on Lamarckism. Repr. in P. Medawar (Ed.), The uniqueness of the individual (pp. 63–87). New York: Dover.

Mehta, B., & Schaal, S. (2002). Forward models in visuomotor control. Journal of Neurophysiology, 88, 942–953.

Mesoudi, A. (2008). Foresight in cultural evolution. *Biological Philosophy*, 23, 243–255.

Mesoudi, A. (2011). Cultural evolution: How Darwinian theory can explain human culture and synthesize the social sciences. Chicago: University of Chicago Press.

Mesoudi, A. (2015). Pursuing Darwin's curious parallel: Prospects for a science of cultural evolution. Proceedings of the National Academy of Sciences, 114, 7853–7860.

Moulton, S. T., & Kosslyn, S. M. (2009). Imagining predictions: Mental imagery as mental emulation. Philosophical Transactions of the Royal Society B, 364, 1273–1280.

Pezzulo, G., Butz, M. V., Castelfranchi, C., & Falcone, R. (Eds.). (2008). Anticipation in natural and artificial cognition. In G. Pezzulo, M. Butz, C. Castelfranchi, The challenge of anticipation: A unifying framework for the analysis and design of artificial cognitive systems, (pp. 3–22). New York: Springer.

Pinker, S. (2002). The blank slate: *The modern denial of human nature*. New York: Penguin.

Plotkin, H. (2011). Human nature, cultural diversity and evolutionary theory. Philosophical Transactions of the Royal Society Series B, 366, 454–463.

Rao, R. P., & Ballard, D. H. (1999). Predictive coding in the visual cortex: A functional interpretation of some extra-classical receptive-field effects. Nature Neuroscience, 2, 79–87. doi: 10.1038/4580.

Rescorla, R. A., & Wagner, A. R. (1972). A theory of Pavlovian conditioning: Variations in the effectiveness of reinforcement and nonreinforcement. In A. H. Black, & W. F. Prokasy (Eds.), Classical conditioning II: Current research and theory (pp. 64–99). New York: Appleton Century Crofts.

Richerson, P. J., & Boyd, R. (2005). Not by genes alone: How culture transformed human evolution. Chicago: University of Chicago Press.

Schacter, D. L., & Addis, D. R. (2009). On the nature of medial temporal lobe contributions to the constructive simulation of future events. Philosophical Transactions of the Royal Society B: Biological Sciences, 364, 1245–1253. doi:10.1098/rstb.2008.0308.

Schooler, J. W., & Dougal, S. (1999). Why creativity is not like the proverbial typing monkey. Psychological Inquiry, 10, 351–356.

Schubotz, R. I. (2007). Prediction of external events with our motor system: Towards a new framework. Trends in Cognitive Sciences, 11, 211–218. doi: 10.1016/j.tics.2007.02.006.

Schultz, W. (2000). Multiple reward signals in the brain. Neuroscience, 1, 199–207.

Simonton, D. K. (1999). Creativity as blind variation and selective retention: Is the creative process Darwinian? Psychological Inquiry, 10, 309–328.

Simonton, D. K. (2007). The creative process in Picasso's Guernica sketches: Monotonic improvements or nonmonotonic variation. *Creativity Research Journal*, 19, 329–344.

Simonton, D. K. (2010). Creative thought as blind-variation and selective-retention: Combinatorial models of exceptional creativity. *Physics of Life Reviews*, 7, 156–179. doi:10.1016/j.plrev.2010.02.002

Smith, E. A. (2013). Agency and adaptation: New directions in evolutionary anthropology. Annual Review of Anthropology, 41, 103–120.

Sternberg, R. J. (1998). Cognitive mechanisms in human creativity: Is variation blind or sighted? Journal of Creative Behavior, 32, 159–176.

Thelen, E., & Smith, L. B. (2006). Dynamic systems theories. In R. M. Lerner, & W. Damon (Eds.), *Handbook of child psychology: Theoretical models of human development* (6th ed., pp. 258–312). Hoboken, NJ: John Wiley & Sons.

Tennebaum, J. B., Kemp, C., Griffiths, T. L., & Goodman, N. D. (2011). How to grow a mind: Statistics, structure and abstraction. Science, 331, 1279–1285.

Tonegawa, S. (1983). Somatic generation of antibody diversity. Nature, 302, 575.

Tsao, J. Y., Ting, C. L., & Johnson, C. M. (2019). Creative outcome as implausible utility. Review of General Psychology, 23, 279–292.

Weisberg, R. W. (2004). On structure in the creative process: A quantitative case-study of the creation of Picasso's Guernica. Empirical Studies of the Arts, 22, 23–54.

Weisberg, R. W., & Hass, R. (2007). We are all partly right: Comment on Simonton. Creativity Research Journal, 19, 345–360.

Wolpert, D. M., Doya, K., & Kawato, M. (2003). A unifying computational framework for motor control and social interaction. Philosophical Transactions of the Royal Society Series B, 358, 593–602.

Wolpert, D. M., & Ghahramani, Z. (2000). Computational principles of movement neuroscience. Nature Neuroscience, 3, 1212–1228.

Wolpert, D. M., Ghahramani, Z., & Jordan, M. I. (1995). An internal model for sensorimotor integration. Science, 269, 1880–1882.

Cambridge Elements ≡

Creativity and Imagination

Anna Abraham
University of Georgia, USA

Anna Abraham, Ph.D. is the E. Paul Torrance Professor at the University of Georgia, USA. Her educational and professional training has been within the disciplines of psychology and neuroscience, and she has worked across a diverse range of academic departments and institutions the world over, all of which have informed her cross-cultural and multidisciplinary focus. She has penned numerous publications including the 2018 book, *The Neuroscience of Creativity* (Cambridge University Press), and 2020 edited volume, *The Cambridge Handbook of the Imagination*. Her latest book is *The Creative Brain: Myths and Truths* (2024, MIT Press).

About the Series
Cambridge Elements in Creativity and Imagination publishes original perspectives and insightful reviews of empirical research, methods, theories, or applications in the vast fields of creativity and the imagination. The series is particularly focused on showcasing novel, necessary and neglected perspectives.

Cambridge Elements ⁼

Creativity and Imagination

Elements in the Series

Printed in the United States
by Baker & Taylor Publisher Services